Praise

'This book offers you a fast track to strategies that have been proven time and time again. Dominic has an unmatched ability to quickly find, harvest, assess and test ideas and methodologies from great minds all over the world.'
— **Barnaby Lashbrooke**, CEO, timeetc.com

'I recommend this book for all leadership teams that want to cut the crap and go for growth. Dominic gets right to the heart of growth metrics in a simple and tactical way, explaining how getting clear on your mission, having the right A-players on the team, and ensuring you have an open and psychologically safe place to talk as a leadership team are the keys to unlock significant growth potential. After reading this book, I went through a huge company restructure. Dominic's advice helped me to make decisions I wasn't sure about. He helped me gain the confidence to step up and take my company to the next level.'
— **Goiko Llobet**, CEO, growproexperience.com

'I enjoyed reading this book and appreciated the inclusion of all the insightful tools and frameworks that we came to employ in New Signature, after working with Dominic. You don't have to use all of them, just the ones that work for your business. We found the freedom to communicate and act, which was empowering. And we had far fewer (and quicker) internal meetings. I've since founded Qualyfi, a talent development company, and have taken the ideas forward because I know they work. If you want to tackle the real problems in your business, with the added benefit of fostering a great team culture, then I highly recommend this book.

— **Neil Marley**, CEO, qualyfi.co.uk

'As a long-established, family-owned business, we know our stuff. Dominic's book has helped us improve and refocus our long-term vision for SCC. In doing this, we have better engagement with our people, our customers and our communities, with measurable transformation in a short space of time.'

— **James Rigby**, CEO, scc.com

MIND YOUR
F**KING
BUSINESS

The no-nonsense guide to
making your good business great

DOMINIC MONKHOUSE

R^ethink

First published in Great Britain in 2023
by Rethink Press (www.rethinkpress.com)

© Copyright Dominic Monkhouse

To my wife, Geri.
You are the wind beneath my wings.

Contents

Foreword

Most of what we think we know about building a successful business is bullshit.

Don't believe me? I get it. Look at any apparently thriving business from the outside, and it seems to be the product of years of well-planned and executed decisions, wisdom and expertise.

The truth is most businesses are built in a very different way. They're cobbled together, piece by piece, into a sketchy patchwork of outdated thinking, decades-old management principles and untested methodologies.

Game-changing decisions – far from being carefully thought through – tend to be made emotionally, in the heat of the moment, while leaders are facing tremendous problems and challenges. And even when they're not, changes are still often based on nothing more than assumptions or hunches and hastily executed against a backdrop of immense time and resource pressures.

As leaders, we're surrounded by an almost never-ending deluge of 'content' – mostly of dubious quality – telling us what we should be doing and how we should be doing it. It's so easy to find answers to our business problems with a quick Google, that we've stopped questioning and testing what we're reading and implementing into our businesses.

I should know. For the past twenty years I've been building businesses by feeling my way as best I can, cobbling together the knowledge I need to reach the next level or to break through yet another barrier to growth. During that time, I've had to learn how to manage my time, find and look after customers, attract and retain high-performing staff members, and evolve from a scrappy founder to a leader people can trust.

At every stage of growth, I've faced serious challenges and I've had no choice but to meet them in the best way I could at the time – usually by fumbling around blindly for a solution. Somehow, I wonder how I've managed to build a market-leading, profitable company that now employs, or helps find work for, more than 700 people on two continents.

But what if I hadn't had to guess my way through each challenge as it came? How much faster could I have achieved the same result, or perhaps even something much more remarkable? How many hundreds of hours could I have saved myself? What if I needn't have gone through all the stress I encountered along the way?

This book offers you the opportunity to potentially save yourself years' worth of trial and error, of making decisions under extreme stress and having to see for yourself – through the grim reality of making mistakes – how hard it really is to build a scalable, profitable and successful business that people truly love to work for.

You picked up this book because you already know that the way you're trying to scale your business isn't working the way you want it to. And the following chapters offer a fresh perspective and clear path forward. Instead of having to battle each growth challenge as it comes, you'll benefit from the decades of real experience Dominic has gathered during his years at the helm of high-growth global tech businesses like Rackspace and Peer1.

I first met Dominic years ago when we were both thrust into the world of a high-growth tech giant in the midst of a fast and well-funded acquisition spree, buying up UK hosting and broadband companies like mine. I was a young entrepreneur who found myself, briefly, in the corporate world after selling my first business, and Dominic – then my new boss – was a seasoned leader who'd worked his way up from shop assistant at Marks & Spencer to managing director of the company's hosting division.

Dominic is a strong leader, excellent salesman and even better people person, and this book would surely prove very valuable if it were just based on his experiences alone – but it isn't. The thing that makes Dominic unique is his unmatched ability to quickly find, harvest, assess and test ideas and methodologies from great minds all over the world. In short, this book offers you a fast-track to strategies that have been proven time and time again.

When I deployed the strategies, insights and ideas in this book in my own business, I felt like a weight had been lifted from my shoulders. Within months of implementing the Net Promoter Score system for our clients, we saw our client retention increase, almost overnight, by more than it had done in years. Likewise, when we switched from having managers to coaches and from annual reviews to monthly one-to-ones we saw our employee engagement leap so high that we scored in the top 1% of all companies worldwide in the renowned Gallup Employee Engagement index.

I noticed something else about the strategies in this book too: they really stick. Gone are the days when we'd flipflop from one strategy to another, desperately trying to get our team to adopt them and run with it. There's something about these strategies that makes them easy to implement *and* to keep. In fact, I was so delighted with the results, I asked Dominic if he would coach our leadership team as we strived to reach the next level of growth.

By picking up this book you've already embarked on an exciting journey towards sustainable growth in your business. Implement the strategies contained within this book and I promise you, you won't be disappointed with the results.

Barnaby Lashbrooke
Founder and CEO at virtual assistant platform
Time etc, https://web.timeetc.com
Author of productivity manual *The Hard Work Myth*, https://hardworkmyth.com

Introduction

Every week, I speak to entrepreneurial CEOs of fast-growing businesses with seemingly insurmountable problems. I wrote this book for them. Maybe you feel the same way? In which case, I wrote this book for you.

At the root of these insurmountable problems are myths or beliefs about how things 'should' be done. They become embedded as habits and ways of operating. And they hold businesses back. Too often, business leaders are trying to reinvent the wheel. They're making it hard for themselves. I'm here to tell you it doesn't need to be this complicated.

It reminds me of a podcast conversation between two medics. They're discussing the amount of time it takes for a piece of primary research to become common practice. Their conclusion? Fifteen to twenty years. It takes that long to change people's minds and perceptions. And sometimes, these perceptions aren't even based on fact. One medic said, 'I used to believe I needed to take baby aspirin to avoid DVT before I flew anywhere. But when one of my researchers searched for evidence to back this up, there wasn't any!'[1]

In the same way, the things you believe are non-negotiable in your business might not be based on any supporting evidence. Maybe you use annual appraisals for performance management. Why? Is there any evidence to show they increase engagement or productivity? Perhaps you also feel you always need to pay salespeople commission? You don't! Just because it's what other businesses do, doesn't make it right for you.

My challenge to you as you read this book is to ask questions. Question your biases and your beliefs. Get curious. Do your research. Because often, the things you believe to be true are not based on fact. They may be the result of 'groupthink'.

This book will help you challenge your assumptions and demystify some of the barriers to business growth. Each chapter deals with the most common self-imposed obstacles I see when coaching business leaders. They revolve around sales, customers, talent acquisition, employer brand, appraisals, leadership, culture and values. The book is brimming with tools and practical methods to provide actionable insights into how to run your business effectively.

If your company has hit an inflection point or your growth has stalled, the information I share in this book should give you an understanding of the underlying issues you're facing and the courage to push through to achieve your goals for your company.

The words of Marshall Goldsmith come to mind here. 'What got you here will not get you there.'[2] Leadership teams must challenge their existing beliefs to grow through these inflection points and continue the journey. This book provides the data and evidence to see beyond what you 'know' but haven't yet challenged. You'll need to grow as a leader and make sweeping changes to how you operate your business.

If you're dissatisfied with the status quo at work, this book is for you. Whether you're a team leader looking for more meaning in your job or a CEO struggling to build a positive culture, understand there is a better way, and I'm here to show you it. I've been in jobs where every day's a grind. It's pure misery! But when you reach the end of this book, you'll sense the possibilities for the future.

At the very least, I hope that reading this will bring you back some joy in your work. It should inspire you to strive for better. There are plenty of businesses out there that use the methods I'm about to describe. You'll find them in any of the 'Best Places to Work' award lists. Your current role may give you the influence to create a culture that's worthy of this list. Or maybe the things I've mentioned resonate so deeply that you'll ditch your current employer and apply to join one of these great companies. Best of all, my advice isn't rocket science. It's easy to implement and follow through.

How do I know this stuff? Because I've been there. The companies I've managed have won multiple awards – I'm proud to have built great places to work. As managing director, I scaled two UK technology companies from zero revenue to £30 million in five years. This is how I learned the execution systems that work, made many mistakes, and discovered innovative strategies that disrupted competitors.

I now coach entrepreneurial CEO clients and their teams to solve problems with their people and culture. It always comes back to those two things. And this book isn't about having a great culture just for the sake of it. It's about building a culture that drives high performance.

In April 2018, I started a weekly blog, newsletter and podcast, aiming to demystify growth for entrepreneurial CEOs, MDs and business leaders. What is holding leaders back is already known. My purpose is to make this knowledge more accessible. We haven't missed a week of sharing since the podcast began. I'm on a mission to enrich the lives of our community. When blog readers and podcast listeners contact me and tell me of their success having read or listened to my advice, it's hugely rewarding. This book encapsulates my best advice to give you the chance to reap successes like theirs.

Lastly, the words I most often hear from my clients and audience members are, 'Why hasn't someone told me this before?' I'm here to tell you, so keep reading.

1
Finding, Building And Motivating A Successful Sales Team

Two of the most transformative lessons I have learned from serving as a change agent dedicated to delivering explosive growth relate to decision-making, motivation, money and sales, and how these interconnect.

The first lesson is as simple as it is powerful: people rarely make decisions based solely on logic or common sense. Purchase decisions – including those made by corporate buyers – tend to be influenced, sometimes disproportionately, by temporary feelings and emotional triggers.

The second lesson is linked to the first, but most people experience it as being counterintuitive. It is this: sales professionals are rarely primarily motivated by money. While fat bonuses and commissions might initially drive sales performance, they need to have other motivation elsewhere if they are to achieve sustained excellence.

To check the credibility of these two lessons, you need only look into how the commission-based compensation scheme for sales professionals works. At first glance, the rationale seems rock solid. After all, most people do desire varying degrees of financial gain, security or comfort. Not surprisingly, recruiters, talent managers and sales leaders buy in to the conventional wisdom that successful salespeople are motivated primarily by money. According to the commission-driven mindset, the potential to acquire hefty bonuses will motivate sales professionals not only to meet quotas, but also to go the extra mile consistently. This is pretty much the ideal scenario for an organisation and all the people in its revenue engine.

As a result, many companies embrace a commission-driven compensation strategy for their sales teams. For starters, offering commission has become a handy excuse for expense-wary organisations to justify low basic pay for sales professionals. While the arguments for the practice sound reasonable (eg 'It fairly distributes risk between worker and employer,' 'It makes everyone accountable for performance,' etc), the reality in the sales team is different. Indeed, real-world data says just the opposite. Most salespeople fail to achieve their quotas, even when the monetary incentive to do so is high.[3] The primary motivation, financial gain, is always within reach, but quota attainment remains elusive for sales teams across the board.[4] Just think of the following – if paying for performance worked, then tips in bars and restaurants would consistently result in excellent service.

Other factors positively affect sales performance, not least of which is the amount of time sales professionals spend doing non-selling tasks such as updating CRM data, answering queries on emails, and providing customer care. Prospecting – the arduous process of finding potential customers – can itself consume large chunks of your sales team's time and energy.

But even with highly specialised roles (more on this later), a commission-based culture doesn't fully explain why rock-star salespeople perform the way they do. Except for some professions such as stock trading, monetary gain does not fully account for exceptional performance. Human psychology does.

This principle and many others are explored in convention-defying books on business hacking and behavioural economics. Daniel H Pink's *Drive: The surprising truth about what motivates us* and Jim Collins' *Good to Great: Why some companies make the leap... and others don't* readily come to mind. In the field of sales, this reality is explored by Justin Roff-Marsh in his book, *The Machine: A radical approach to the design of the sales function.*[5]

Numerous researchers in behavioural science have shown that human achievement and creativity require high levels of engagement and motivation.[6] The trouble is, we have been looking for motivation in the wrong places. Studies conducted at Massachusetts Institute of Technology (MIT) and other academic institutions have revealed that monetary rewards in the form of bonuses and higher pay drive better performance only in tasks that require basic mechanical skills.[7] In contrast, higher incomes for jobs that involve creativity, strategic thinking and solving complicated problems unexpectedly resulted in poor performance.

Author Daniel H Pink argues that humans who succeed in professions that require deep cognitive skills are 'intrinsically motivated' and are less affected by external factors. His argument debunks the longstanding – and unfortunately still prevalent – belief that motivation is driven by a reward–punishment system, as found in the modern workplace with lower basic wages paired with generous bonuses, commissions and other financial incentives. Exceptionally successful people find from within themselves a deeper form of motivation, whose core aspects are autonomy, mastery, and purpose.

This book attempts to shatter misconceptions about processes and people, and to replace or update business mindsets that are already stale but have become entrenched over time. Resistance always precedes change, and I understand letting go of cherished mantras and embracing new ones can be difficult. But adopting new ideas can bring great rewards, so keep an open mind as you read on.

Sales superstars don't need commission to shine

I advise executives not to pay salespeople commission – pay them reasonable salaries instead.

This goes against the grain in many organisations, but it aligns well with the science behind human nature and human potential. If your company offers a great solution that salespeople believe in, they'll be glad to sell it. And they'll do so for a salary without additional financial incentive, because they're accomplishing something useful, meaningful, and purposeful.

After all, if the product will benefit customers, why would you still need to incentivise a decent sales-person to sell it? Intrinsically motivated people will always sell for the right reasons. The best salespeople approach and enjoy selling like a game. They thrive at their craft when they think it's beneficial for their customers to have the solution they're offering.

By the same token, commission works only when a company needs to force professionals to sell an objectionable product or something they don't believe in. In this context, companies use sales commission as a stick (fear), not as a carrot (reward). Unfortunately, bad things happen when workers perform their tasks out of fear. When salespeople are in constant stress, their focus and efficiency drop, while their creativity and other sophisticated skills become less potent.

In fairness, money can generate activity, especially when it comes to manual tasks that require little thought. This encapsulates the difference between transactional selling and solution selling. If all it takes to make a sale is to peddle a product and issue a receipt, then go ahead and offer commission. Research shows, however, that further monetary reward hampers creativity instead of driving it.[8] And because it takes creativity and other advanced cognitive skills to succeed in high-value sales, in this environment, the sales force needs to be rewarded differently.

Another factor to consider is the fact that the salesperson is rarely the only one speaking with a prospective customer. Usually, someone in presales creates the initial solution for the prospect. If a salesperson earns a commission for landing the deal, this often creates tension with those non-sales people who helped bring the deal into existence. Replacing commission with a salary would remove this tension completely.

How to find and motivate the right salespeople

Not paying salespeople commission begs a couple of follow-up questions: what is a reasonable salary?

And how exactly do you find the right kind of sales professionals?

As a rule of thumb, the salary should be sufficient for salespeople to feel assured that their basic needs are met and that they are receiving fair compensation. Otherwise, inadequate pay will persistently distract members of your sales team, diminishing their drive, and crippling the creativity needed to solve customer problems.

The idea is to offer an attractive salary that will keep salespeople focused on customer engagement instead of obsessing over quota attainment. Because a good salary squarely addresses a sales professional's own financial challenges, they can exert optimal effort to help customers solve theirs. Which, incidentally, is the best approach to winning deals, getting referrals and maximising clients' lifetime value. Even the best salespeople can take up to twelve months to reach their sales quota.[9]

Meanwhile, finding and keeping the right type of salespeople for your business is a matter of under-standing how motivation happens and building a sales culture that cultivates and unleashes human potential. Few executives fully grasp the true nature of how salespeople are motivated, and even fewer act based on such insight. Recruiters and sales lead-ers who dangle hefty commissions to attract top employees or drive team performance can expect painful disappointment down the line. On the other side of the coin, sales professionals whose primary motivation sounds like a cash register won't find true fulfilment in a sales-centric career.

Here are three essential and unashamedly unconventional steps you can take as a business owner or sales leader to recruit the right people for your team:

1. Never focus on financial incentives to motivate salespeople.

2. Hire salespeople who are already motivated. Look for drive. Find people who are intrinsically driven.

3. Craft job ads that resonate with your ideal candidate's intrinsic motivations.

Understanding your candidates' motivations

Staffing your revenue engine with people who are self-motivated instead of money-driven is the key to sales success. But how exactly do you find them?

Here's one question that will help you reveal the core motivation of a job candidate. I didn't come up with this question – Jill Garret, Tentpeg Consulting executive director and former Gallup managing director, came up with it, and kindly allowed me to quote her here. I've asked this question umpteen times in job interviews. Every time, the job candidate's answer is illuminating. Here it is:

'What was your best deal? Tell me all about it.'

When asked to describe their best deal, a financially driven salesperson will most likely mention their largest deal or the biggest commission they have earned. They are not the seller you want.

Intrinsically motivated professionals describe the deal that posed the most formidable challenge, cut the deepest, gave the most profound lesson, or made them feel the proudest. The cream of the crop will talk about how their best deal created a great result for their customer. That's the main point, though they may also tell you how they identified and solved the customer's problem, describing the epic efforts, unique tactics, and the great lengths it took them just to win the deal.

The finest salespeople are problem solvers. Extremely curious, they ask a lot of questions. They empathise with the customer and seek to understand their pain points. They visualise solutions and draw new connections for the client.

Selling is *not* order taking. The seller has to believe the customer will be better off if they purchase. The selling is in the customer coming to the same realisation.

How to create a killer job ad

Crafting resonant job ads is another method you can use to draw the right salespeople to your team. Make strong connections with top-notch talent by focusing on their aspirations. This is where you can take action based on the core aspects of human motivation: autonomy, mastery and purpose.[10]

Outstanding sales professionals aspire to be the best in their field. They love selling and want to master their craft. They are passionate about helping people and find purpose in their career. They are proud of their profession and will showcase their achievements in their CVs. Influence and respect are the two things that matter most to sales superstars.[11]

Look for salespeople who crave mastery, professionals who want to be excellent at selling. These elite sellers proactively gain new knowledge and develop skills to get better at what they already do very well. You won't find them saying, 'I've been in sales for twenty years, and I've learned everything I'll ever need.' Instead, they'll seek opportunities where they can have more autonomy or elevate their mastery of the trade. These top sellers are proud of who they are and are seeking somewhere they can get even better at selling.

If you want to attract and hire such talent, highlight what's in it for them in your ad's first paragraph.

Avoid using your bragging rights (even if you have them) to tell irrelevant stories about your company. A job ad for top-tier sales talent should be about them, not about you.

You are aiming for performers who regularly hit at least 110% of their sales targets or who make it to the President's Club many years in a row. This is a very select group of people. According to Steve W Martin in 'A portrait of the overperforming salesperson', top sales professionals are those who achieved more than 125% of their quota from the previous year, and only 15% of the 1,000 salespeople and sales management leaders in Martin's study met this criterion.[12]

In the job ad, talk about how people in your team enjoy more autonomy, gain mastery of their craft or discover a deeper purpose in their career. Focus on the employees' challenges and make the candidate notice how you can make them even more awesome. Minimise the BS about your company, or just get rid of it altogether.

Post personal and targeted questions like the following:

- Are you struggling to meet your life goals by staying in a business that is stifling your own ambition?

- When was the last time you learned something new and effective from your sales manager?

- Are you a natural salesperson with great skills? Are you frustrated in your current role?

- Does your current employer lack ambition or real competitive edge?

Questions like these resonate with top performers. They think to themselves, 'How did they know I was feeling unchallenged?'

You also need to think about the emotional drivers that motivate the kind of candidates you're looking for. What makes them strive for excellence? What stresses them out? What factors are compelling them to change employers and what will entice them to join my company?

Visualise a talented salesperson after another frustrating week. It's Sunday night, their laptop's on their knee, glass of wine in hand, and they're checking out some job ads as the prospect of yet another frustrating work week hits them. You want them to notice your opportunity, and you want to build a connection with them. Remember, their problem is not usually money, so don't attempt to attract them by saying, 'Come here and earn more money.'

You want them to be so affected by your messaging that they apply the moment they see it. When you do get their attention, however, make sure to convince them that they can get better at what they've decided to spend the rest of their lives doing. Only then will the very best people join your company.

Note: it's not always possible to get top-tier talent in your team. It might be that your brand or product doesn't have the same draw as others in your space. You might have some steep budgetary constraints. Or more likely, the finest sales professionals in your industry already enjoy VIP treatment at the leading companies in your market. If any of this applies to you, hire sales talent from adjacent sectors or industries. B2B sales across verticals and sectors share common denominators. And always hire for attitude and intrinsic motivation. Product knowledge and skills training can come later.

Practical tips for building your sales team

If sales success could be distilled into a formula, then it would be a function of people, process, product, and perspective (culture). How you build and bind these elements would determine how efficiently you could sustain strong growth.

It takes the right kind of salespeople working within the right kind of culture to tip the human side of the equation in your favour. But that's just half the battle. It also takes a well-designed product and a stream-lined process to close the loop.

Here are some practical tips and tactics to consider when building a superstar sales team.

Hire sales rock stars

Look for the right personality traits and motivation at the hiring stage. The best sales professionals are resourceful. If you only hire for one attribute, make it resourcefulness. These candidates own everything and never blame other people. They are particularly hard on themselves. They will go above and beyond to close a deal. They aim for a 100% close rate because they shun writing proposals for people who aren't going to buy. Instead, they write order forms – simply because nobody has ever been persuaded to buy anything by a proposal. Ever.

There's an interesting study that correlated five personality profiles with 1,000 successful salespeople, aiming to answer once and for all whether great salespeople are born or made.[13] It turns out that 70% are born self-driven, while 30% are motivated by money. If you're not born a great salesperson but crave money, you might force yourself to work hard enough to get there.

Unfortunately, most people consider the 30% as the archetypal sales superstar. Think of the Hollywood stereotype – they drive flashy cars and exhibit annoying levels of arrogance. Because of confirmation bias, even executives and companies seek out these money-driven salespeople.

But again, most people aren't motivated by money all the time. Software developers won't write better code if you pay them per line of code. Nor would customer service reps provide better service if you pay them per ticket. Instead, we can use Net Promoter Scores to measure results/performance (for more on NPS see Chapter Two).

Here is my list of common traits of exceptional salespeople:

- They are modest. Instead of showcasing themselves, they position the sales team to do the deal.

- They control the sales cycle.

- They are achievement oriented.

- They measure their performance. Their CV contains percentage vs quota for every role.

- They fixate on the results of their customers, not on the results of the products.

- They are curious. They read and learn continuously.

- They are not gregarious, brash or in your face.

- They know how to lose, but they'll fight to win. They love to win.

- They practise. How many of your sales team practise? The best performers practise every day.

- They are unaware of their rarity and have no idea that most people on the planet are not like them.

Designing a product

It takes excellence and authenticity to achieve true success. When it comes to your product or service, mediocrity won't go very far with either the people who'll sell them or the customers who'll use them. A great product will make your salespeople feel good trying to win deals. And great service will keep your customers from switching brands.

In every sector, there's only ever one firm that can be the biggest, or the cheapest, or the best (whatever 'best' means). The only way to compete is to have a unique strategy. So, really, you don't need to be the biggest, the cheapest, or the best at anything. You just have to be unique or effective at solving specific customer problems. At the very least, your product or service should provide such value or benefit to customers that you'll never need to incentivise salespeople to sell it.

Your sales proposition can be tightened by narrowing your target audience to the subset of your market who can use your product to improve their lives/business. When your top salespeople know this, they'll be happy selling and helping customers.

Jim Collins' Hedgehog Concept serves as a good template for designing your product.[14] You can apply it to discover your ideal craft or the speciality your business should be known for. The Hedgehog Concept involves the intersection of three circles, each of which represents a key question you should ask yourself or your product team:

1. What are you deeply passionate about?
2. What can you be the best in the world at?
3. What drives your economic engine?

You'll be on the right track if you allow these questions to guide your product management, sales and go-to-market strategies.

Note that some companies have neither a superior product nor a crack team of elite sellers. Yet they still succeed by being the only consistently reliable company in the market known for providing a hyper-specific service.

A good example is a global IT service firm that took a British-built 4x4 company to China. With China's massive bureaucracy and regulatory regime acting like a firewall for doing business in the country, this company's expertise in helping multinationals gain a foothold in the mainland provided value for brands looking to enter the Chinese market.

When I consulted with this company, I said, 'Your route to market is to approach CIOs of large UK businesses. Ask them, "You're not in China, do you want to go there? We can help you do that and manage your IT from here. Would you like to hear how we did that for a British-built 4x4 company?" What happens next will be conversations where sales kick in.' This exercise helped the company realise its future state: how it would help businesses through a difficult and specific challenge no one else was good at navigating.

Once you have a full grasp of this future state for your business, you can get closer to your goal by taking the right actions and making the necessary changes today. It will also help you clarify your purpose. When you can offer customers a specialised product or service, you can build a unique proposition and strategy. You don't need to be the biggest or cheapest. You just need to know how your product benefits target clients. When you reach this point, your salespeople will move as if they're on a mission. They won't be selling anything they don't believe in. On the contrary, they would be helping to solve a problem they know your customers struggle with.

When you proactively build your product or service to be specific and useful, your team acquires a worthy purpose – they gain the ability and motivation to make a difference.

Focus and specialisation

If you asked a group of hoteliers how they could double their revenue, they'd likely respond with suggestions such as:

- 'Double the number of guests booking rooms.'

- 'Double the number of rooms.'

- 'Double the price per booking.'

They'd make these kinds of 'logical' suggestions, even when they know that in practice, things are a lot more complicated. Scaling a business is of course not as easy as it sounds.

Would you double your revenue if you doubled your sales team? Business insiders will answer 'No' outright. Some will give an estimate, say a 25% revenue increase. Not many people with experience would say 'Yes.' Just about everyone is willing to accept that doubling the number of salespeople won't double the revenue – if it did, we would do it instantly. It is not only that most sales organisations are not designed with scalability in mind, but also that salespeople are not adequately motivated, don't contribute proportionately to business results, or simply aren't selling the way they should.

When I ask executives such questions, they realise for themselves, rather than from me telling them, that they haven't been running their sales operations as optimally as they could. Then they're compelled to round up management and the CEO to analyse what they've been doing to motivate their current sales team. Almost always, they arrive at the same conclusion: they could probably double their sales if they just double the duration that salespeople are selling. But to achieve that, you have to systematically chip away every single excuse for not selling. And you have to start thinking about focus and specialisation.

You need people who excel at the specific tasks they enjoy doing. If you can build a process supported by clearly defined specialist roles, then you can scale the company. You can't scale the company using generalists.[15] You simply have to keep the people who can actually perform their specific roles exceptionally well and get rid of those who can't.

Finding specialist sellers should be top of your agenda. They're easy to spot but rare. They're on a mission. They're not trying to sell customers something they don't want. Instead, they help solve their problems. If you can make these specialist sales professionals find purpose in what your company offers, then it becomes easier to hire the best people, manage a high-performing team, and scale the business.

Case in point: one of our clients employs a phenomenal salesperson who sucks at administrative tasks such as booking meetings and filling up forms. This guy has dismal proficiency in Salesforce and would flunk any test on CRM competency even if his life depended on it. But my client knows that this person is so exceptional at the role they hired him for – actual selling – that they decided to give him his own personal assistant. He no longer does any admin tasks himself. He focuses solely on what he does best. They don't care about the extra expense of the PA's salary.

Justin Roff-Marsh says exactly the same thing: focus on strengths, not weaknesses. When you have a great salesperson, you give her a personal assistant. Why would you want her to do her own admin? Or her own expenses for that matter? If you've got a really talented sales professional, you just want her to do the thing she's amazing at, nothing else.

Building a process

Here's a common conversation I've had with many prospective clients who then became actual clients.

Business leader: [Optimistic] Hey, Dominic, we'd like you to help us hire a sales guy and put in a sales commission scheme.

Me: I'd like to help. But I don't think you need a commission scheme.

Business leader: [Confused] But how will we manage him?

Me: How do you manage the other people in your business? How do other professionals in your company know what to do day in and day out? To them, what makes a good

day look good? You just need to have the
same stuff in place for the salesperson.

As a sales manager, you need to define and track all
the indicators that help your sales team achieve its
goals. You can simplify this process. Almost always,
business objectives such as sales order income depend
on activity-based metrics, such as the number of calls
per day or number of meetings per week, which you
can adjust to work in your favour.

Here's an example. With a sales cycle that commonly
exceeds one year, a company offering legal IT services wants to double their business. The company's
managing director, Matt, is also the top seller. By all
accounts, all the other salespeople can't pitch better
than Matt, who's been doing it for twenty years.

To win deals, Matt needs to sit down with senior
partners in prospective law firms. Based on their pro-
jections, it will take at least one pitch per week for
Matt to achieve their target growth.

We can easily conclude that Matt's expertise lies in
closing deals. That's what he enjoys and excels at
doing. Because Matt exudes confidence in this role,
prospects trust him. We'll narrow his role to the specialist function of deal closer. At the same time, we'll
hire a sales opener, whose task is to engage prospects
and put at least one potential customer in a room
with Matt each week. That support salesperson will

perform all the other phases in the sales cycle apart from closing.

Matt hires a new salesperson to prospect, open doors and book closing meetings. The new salesperson does all the time-consuming admin. This frees up Matt to do his other job of being managing director and running the company. They grow and sell the business. Now Matt coaches other business leaders on how to do this themselves.

We'll pay everyone a reasonable salary, not commission. If you pay via commission, the money is likely to be principally accumulated by the closers. This creates resentment among the other team members, who do much of the work. Instead, business owners and sales leaders should work out what they think a particular job is worth and then pay a great salary.

As Justin Roff-Marsh found, you do not want to pay a per-piece rate if you want to re-engineer your sales process into a well-oiled machine. You'll get greater productivity by paying everybody a salary and getting everyone to collaborate. And you will have highly skilled specialists at all elements of the operation.

The key takeaway is this: specialisation is key. All tasks that are non-sales shouldn't be done by salespeople. Remember, the definition of a salesperson is the rare individual who is great at and loves selling and can move a deal forwards to close. When roles are properly specialised, the business can scale more easily, with the contribution of new salespeople roughly reflected as net new revenue. Using this framework, salespeople only sell. They don't provide customer service, send quotes or update CRM data. They don't even generate opportunities. They just sell. And you pay them a salary for doing that.

If you follow an account-based framework, I advise that you take away and reassign one-third of an account executive's portfolio every year, replacing it with customers from other account managers. This keeps things fresh, and it's amazing how many times we have seen sales come from customers the previous account manager wasn't able to sell to. This can spell the difference between a stagnant and a growing company.

Blending all the parts into a winning culture

As a growing number of industries adopt the metrics that gauge employee satisfaction and engagement, more and more companies have realised the crucial importance of culture to the sustainability and relevance of their brands. In my stints as an executive at Peer 1 Hosting (now Aptum Technologies), Rackspace, and other companies, I made sure we weren't only hacking business growth but also transforming organisational culture. As a result, many of the companies I led won coveted awards and often ranked among the best places to work in the UK and Europe.[16]

You have to create a sales culture that inspires awesome people to show up when you expect them to. You have to orchestrate a work environment and work experiences that compel staff to gladly use more of their discretionary effort.[17]

In sales as much as in other fields, the best culture is one specifically designed to unleash human potential. You don't have to financially motivate people, but you do have to generate genuine excitement about your brand, your mission and your purpose. It's all about the balance of trust in and empowerment of your people to give their best performance every time.

Summary

- Purchasing decisions are rarely made logically and often made emotionally.

- Money is not the strongest motivator for sales professionals. Your commission-based rewards scheme may be negatively affecting your employees' performance rather than driving it.

- Look to recruit rock-star sales professionals who are already driven, who are intrinsically motivated. Do this by offering an attractive salary (not commission), and by crafting job ads that speak to their emotional needs, not their financial ones.

- Create a killer product using the Hedgehog Concept that a high-performing sales team will love to sell.

- Be strategic about specialisms and assign people's tasks with these in mind – your top salespeople should only be selling. Let someone else take on the tasks they're not as good at.

- Create an inspiring business culture in which your employees can thrive.

2
Building A Customer-centric Culture

Sometimes, bad news is good news.

For customers to love your brand, you need to know what they hate about it, much more than what they like. Only when you have full visibility of unfiltered customer opinion will you have the insight needed to continuously improve your product, sustain customer trust, and drive brand loyalty.

In the age of digital engagement, customer satisfaction as we know it is dead. Customer happiness has become the new battleground. It's no longer enough that customers are satisfied with your product or service. You want them to like it so much that they'll rave about it on online reviews. You want customers to recommend your product or service to their friends on social media. And you'd like them to refer new prospects to your sales development team. In short, you want customers to be promoters in the language of the Net Promoter System (NPS).[18]

As new business competitors emerge, only with enough happy customers can you drive and sustain strong revenue growth. This conclusion is borne out by real-world data and everyday experience – for example, wouldn't you recommend and return to a hotel that gives away all the munchies in a fully packed minibar for free? Ovolo Hotels do exactly that, and I stay with them every chance I get.

Customers have got used to being milked dry of every pound/buck/euro in their pockets by companies who see them as purses, not people. With this being the standard experience, any company that chooses to take a different route will surely get noticed. When a business prioritises customer service, everybody wins.

Exceptional service is the best and most rewarding path towards competitive differentiation. In the airline industry, for example, nearly all players charge a luggage fee. Southwest Airlines doesn't. And people can't help but love them for it. Because Southwest obsesses over customer experience, it strives to lead the race in efficiency and affordability. Doing so enables the Dallas-based low-cost carrier to flourish even during tough economic periods while their competitors are brought to their knees.

Criticism is your friend

Many companies approach customer satisfaction incorrectly. In nearly every market, businesses prioritise profits, and by doing so miss out on valuable opportunities to either a) provide excellent experiences customers will remember or b) rectify bad experiences they won't forget.

Unfortunately, bad experiences, especially when unaddressed, almost always lead to customer churn. Dissatisfied customers will ditch your brand in favour of your competitors. To make matters worse, some of them will rant about their dissatisfaction on social media, effectively launching a negative publicity campaign for your product.

Never ignore customer churn. Left to itself, a runaway churn rate can easily escalate into a death spiral for a business. The reason is simple: it costs a lot more to pick up a new client than to keep an existing one. Depending on your industry, acquiring new customers could range anywhere from five times to twenty-five times the cost of keeping those you already have in your portfolio.[19]

Bain & Company's Frederick Reichheld published a paper in the *Harvard Business Review* that showed a direct link between customer retention rates and corporate profits.[20] According to their research, decreasing churn rate – or increasing customer retention rate – by 5% can increase your profits by 25% to 95%.

Incidentally, this research comes from the author who introduced the concept of Net Promoter System to the business world. Reichheld found that a single question embedded in a customer satisfaction survey can serve as an indicator of company growth: 'How likely are you to recommend our product or service?' The more customers you have who are eager to recommend your brand, the bigger you can grow your business.[21]

Among other things, NPS is about preventing customers from moving to your competitor. That is why you don't gouge people with all sorts of charges, because when some of your customers can move over to your rivals, some of them will. So don't even try to maximise your profit for the short term. If you do, you'll likely just lose out when another company comes along with a better proposition that you can't afford to match.

If you're a decent company, you'll certainly get a lot of positive feedback. That's OK, and it's good to know exactly what you're good at, and which aspects of your offering customers really like. But don't give in to complacency. There's always room for improvement: take the cue from customers to identify exactly where this should be. To achieve this, your organisation needs to be set up to embrace bad news. In fact, you have to deliberately look for it, to gather it both from staff and customers.

Former Intel CEO Andy Grove wrote a fascinating book, *Only the Paranoid Survive: How to exploit the crisis points that challenge every company.*[22] In it, he introduces the idea of a strategic inflection point – a milestone where imminent change can make or break a business. He argues for seeing such points as opportunities to win in the market and become stronger as an organisation. Receiving bad news is an opportunity to drive positive change and improve your brand.

This goes back to Jim Collins' interlocking circles of the Hedgehog Concept in *Good to Great*. In Chapter One, I phrased those three questions in second person ('you') to get you thinking about yourself. Now, I'll rephrase them in first person ('we') to get you thinking about your company:

1. What are we passionate about?

2. What can we be the best in the world at?

3. What can we make money from?

If you want your company to be the best in the world, then you'll need excellent coaches (critics) to conduct post-mortems about your performance. This is the case for all top-notch business teams, just as it is for musical soloists and highly competitive sportspeople. In his autobiography, *OPEN*, Andre Agassi recounts how he battled negative feedback to become one of the greatest tennis players in history.[23] Having started playing tennis as a young prodigy, Agassi managed to thrive within an environment of obstacles and sharp criticisms, going on to win eight Grand Slams over two decades.

Mediocre companies are scared of bad news. The best ones are comfortable with criticism. After all, true confidence grows out of adversity. For business organisations, that means traditional customer satisfaction surveys are out. They are costly, inefficient, and rarely lead to actionable insight.

Instead, ambitious companies must rethink their engagement strategies and go beyond customer feedback. To get ahead of the pack, they must proactively seek criticism. The trouble is, some customers don't want to upset you and will just tell you what you want to hear. To get a more objective picture of customer sentiment, you need to reframe your feedback mechanism and integrate NPS in your customer communications.

Say sorry when you f**k up

There's no perfect product or service. One way or another, at some point in time, something will happen that will frustrate, disappoint or anger your customers. If you don't take action, or fail to make the right moves, customer churn will surely spike.

During these scenarios, conveying that you regret the incident and that you're taking remedial action will help. Words like 'sorry' and 'confess' often help prevent massive customer attrition from happening. When customers see your honesty, they're much more likely to stick with you.

During my years as managing director at Rackspace, one of our business analysts came up with an amazing solution for handling service foul-ups. When a customer experienced a service failure, we apologised and gave them goodwill credits. In short, we'd say sorry and then pay them for the trouble. We kept most of them that way. The opposite also applies: if you're too stiff-necked to say sorry, your customers are more likely to jump ship to one of your rivals.

One particular incident at my former company still stands out for me. Rackspace provides cloud-based data management services to businesses from every sector imaginable. This incident involved a leading business research services company and a major UK bank. The research firm was conducting a staff engagement survey for the bank and was already having challenges dealing with their client. And, in a freakish turn of events during a migration process, Rackspace's data team accidentally fried the database containing the bank's survey information.

I rang up the CTO of the research company and said, 'I'm going to be completely honest. We were troubleshooting stuff and made a major mistake that ruined one of your eighteen databases. It was for the UK-based retail bank. We know that you're already having problems with this company, so please accept our apologies. We are exerting all efforts to recover the data. Not only that, but we conducted other high-availability upgrades and did some staff training to ensure this type of incident won't happen again. In the meantime, we're giving you a £10,000 goodwill credit. I'll also come with you personally to your client [the bank] and explain what happened.'

The CTO replied, 'Look, I doubt if any of my other suppliers would bring up the matter and confess to exactly what happened, and that they've mitigated the issue. Also, I doubt that they would ever come with me to meet the bank. I'm not going to take your money.'

The client appreciated our honesty, declined the goodwill credit and, I understand, still partners with Rackspace to this day. Incidentally, this story evolved into a kind of urban legend and forms part of the NPS-driven culture that still elevates Rackspace above its peers in the industry.

Here's the bottom line: if you screw something up, call the customer and tell them. Most companies don't because they think admitting failure will erode the customer's trust. But for Rackspace, the opposite happened. Customers trusted us more because we were honest. And these days, you rarely find honesty in the business world. To make your outreach more genuine, offer something of real value, like goodwill credits, to fairly compensate the disadvantaged client. Your finance officers and accountants who advocate for profit maximisation might baulk at the idea, but the approach works. When you say sorry and take adequate remedial measures, most customers will stay with you.

Building a customer-centric culture

How, then, do you create and sustain the right culture for your customer-facing teams?

Don't worry. No one is expected to do this overnight. Depending on the maturity of your organisation, you can either take small incremental steps or make radical leaps to transform your approach to customer engagement. Whichever the case, let's look at some key steps to consider.

Adopt the Net Promoter System

There are many systems and metrics for tracking customer satisfaction, but nothing comes close to NPS. Time and time again, positive business outcomes affirm its efficacy. NPS is a stinging slap to traditional customer satisfaction surveys that only seem to feed a company's false sense of greatness. You know the ones – you get to pat yourself on the back, defy reality and say, 'We're not shit.' The truth is, traditional surveys are complicated, take too long to process and don't say much of anything that can help your company grow. What does an arbitrary score of 3.93 mean anyway? Overall, they're a waste of time.

On the other hand, the NPS system is simple. It's basically just one question with a few follow-ups:

On a scale of zero to 10, how likely are you to recommend our company to a friend or colleague?

Customers who choose nine or ten are considered 'promoters', while those who picked zero to six are 'detractors'. Customers who chose sevens and eights are 'passive'. Your company's NPS is the percentage of people who are promoters minus the percentage of people who are detractors.

For example, if 50% of respondents are promoters, 20% are detractors and 30% are passives, your NPS would be $50 - 20 = 30$.

You can add follow-up questions like:

- What made you give us that score?
- Which features do you like/hate the most?

- How can we improve your experience?

- What is the one service feature that will make you happy enough to score us a 10?

With NPS, getting a nine or ten is fantastic. But even receiving low scores can be turned to good use. By refining the follow-up questions, you can identify areas where you can immediately act and dramatically improve customer satisfaction moving forward.

My own experience with itlab affirms the notion that providing a superior customer experience not only makes good business sense, but also drives profitability and clarifies your purpose.

When I joined itlab as managing director in 2007, its market valuation hovered essentially around zero. It was bleeding £65,000 per month and all we had then was three months' worth of money. We needed to reverse the cash flow back to positive within three months, or we'd go out of business.

Our priority was to rebuild the culture and keep the company from drowning into oblivion. We rattled our brains trying to determine the best way to do that amid itlab's dreadful customer service environment. With a dismal NPS of -2, keeping the existing portfolio intact was impossible and closing new business deals was guaranteed to fail. The funny thing was, the people behind the company knew they offered crappy service, and they always expected the type of customer feedback they rightly deserved. So they just stopped getting feedback because it was too depressing.

But in just two years, itlab recovered, and its value skyrocketed to tens of millions. What happened? Here's how the team achieved that amazing feat:

To turn things around, we implemented an NPS-driven customer service strategy. By focusing on and delighting people on both sides of the engagement – customers and staff – we lifted our NPS to +55. Subsequently, the Great Places to Work Institute and *Financial Times* included itlab in its Top 50 Places to Work list.

Through disciplined actions, we were also able to increase prices by 50% while winning new accounts. Profitability moved out of the red zone up to 7%, while the gross margin for services jumped from 50% to 67%. By the time itlab ripened for acquisition a few years later, its value clocked in at around £61 million.

Categorise your customers into segments

Don't fall into the trap of treating all your customers the same way. Accord everyone the same level of respect, but be strategic when it comes to engagement. You can use NPS to identify high-opportunity customers who are likely to receive more service from the company and give more value in return.

When I was at Peer 1, we had around 13,400 customers worldwide. But you know what? We discovered that 60% of our revenue came from the top 4%, roughly 500 customers. We wanted to double their number because doing so would grow our business by 100% in just three years. We decided to focus on this type of customer and ensure that they received exceptional care, service, and attention.

We were surprised to find that resource allocation didn't reflect the proportionate value of each customer segment. It turned out that we were allocating only a tiny fraction of our resources for top customers, while wasting precious resources on low-value customers. We found we had only 6% of employees focused on this top 4%, so we reallocated and brought it up to 16%. It wasn't difficult to balance the equation.

Hire customer service reps from people-facing sectors

Whichever industry your company operates in, hire customer service people who have worked in the retail and hospitality industries, or other customer-oriented sectors. This step can easily be overlooked, but 'wow' moments in business depend on staff seizing the rare opportunities to delight customers. Most of the staff who do this have high empathy. They understand people and human behaviour.

'Wow' moments are the building blocks of what makes a business great. If you provide more 'wow' moments than negative ones, then you're on the path to excellence. But that is rarely the case. At one of my talks, a corporate event, I asked the audience to raise their hands if they had experienced bad service lately. Almost everybody had. Then I asked people to raise their hands if they'd had an amazing customer experience recently. Only a few had. I proceeded to tell my audience the following 'wow' moment that I had experienced recently.

While staying in the Hotel Contessa in San Antonio, Texas, I rang the room service desk and said, 'Maria, there's nothing on the menu that I want. I just want some plain, natural yoghurt and some fruit.'

She said, 'No problem, Mr Monkhouse, let me sort that out for you.'

What I got was about a pint of yoghurt and an enormous bowl of fruit.

The next day, I rang room service again, and it was the same staff member who answered. (When was the last time you rang room service in a hotel and got the same person two days in a row?) Anyway, Maria said, 'Mr Monkhouse. I was worried about yesterday. I thought I'd done exactly what you wanted. But when your plate came down, it looked to me as though you hadn't eaten anything. Did I misunderstand what you wanted?'

I said, 'No, you didn't. It's just you gave me enough food for a family of five for a week.'

And she said, 'Oh, OK. That's fantastic. I was worried that I hadn't sorted that out for you. Let me send you up a smaller plate today.'

So I got another pint of yoghurt and a smaller – though still large – platter of fruit.

The thing that stood out was that Maria was worried that she hadn't done the right thing. Would anybody else have cared at all for something so minor? It seemed that pleasing and delighting customers were in Maria's DNA. People from the retail and hospitality sectors develop this empathy and motivation to serve, and that's why they are great to have on your team.

So that's what I did at Rackspace. Our customer service people didn't come from the IT industry. They came from retail and hospitality. That's because you can't be successful at serving in a bar or restaurant and hate human beings at the same time. Otherwise, you wouldn't do it.

I advise companies to hire staff from people-facing businesses that have been running for a while. These people get a kick out of caring. And that's exactly what you need. You can't train that characteristic, but you want to harness that DNA. It's interesting. This trait shows up in Gallup's CliftonStrengths assessment as 'responsibility' (more on this in Chapter Three). People who make a promise, keep a promise. Many of our tech support or client advocate teams at the businesses I've run have had responsibility as a top-five strength.

Call your customers

One way to sustain a service-oriented culture is to have executives, including those who work in finance, HR, and marketing, talk with a customer at least once per week. This is very important. I recommend that execs initiate the conversation by talking about the wider industry or business in general before focusing on the client. People are more likely to open up if you do it gently. Execs can use the 4Q conversation questions Verne Harnish outlined in his book *Mastering the Rockefeller Habits*:[24]

- What's going on in your industry?

- How are you (or your business) doing?

- Have you heard anything interesting about our competitors?

- How can we help you get more from and be happy with our services?

Make sure everyone performs this task every week. Make a record of all feedback. Assign large strategic accounts to executive-level staff. Have someone oversee and monitor this process every week.

Identify your legends and celebrate your heroes

Laying the groundwork for a service-oriented culture is hard enough, but you have to consistently build on it to keep your momentum. Most people need to be guided towards developing the proper mindset and behaviour, because only a few (like Maria above) have that special service DNA.

Building a culture is a bit like building a religion. You need artefacts, you need rituals, and you need stories. You need myths and legends that everybody knows and can relate to. You have to tell one another the right stories to believe in. There has to be an oral as well as a written history of the organisation.

Who are your organisation's heroes? Rather than thinking of the company's founders, think about the everyday heroes – the ones that other employees relate to. Put people who generate value for your company on a pedestal.

At Rackspace, we had the Employee of the Month Award. We liked to say that the employee needed to be a customer service fanatic to bag the coveted prize. Voted for by the staff and not arbitrated by senior leadership, that was the company's top award. Staff could win the award when somebody caught them doing the right thing that led to a 'wow' moment for the customer.

Meanwhile, at Macquarie, they also apply NPS to service desk staff. If you get ten scores of 10, you become a legend. Then there is a monthly competition called the 'League of Legends', where top service staff compete to be put on the pedestal.

Peer 1 had its own set of heroes. One of its customers, an ecommerce site, lost £100,000 the first day they went live. Their front-end website was taking credit card transactions that weren't coming through to the warehouse, so they had to refund buyers for all of those purchases.

Three guys – including Darius Pieluc and Larry Rye – stayed in the office for three days trying to fix the problems. Nobody asked them to. They simply understood the battering the customers had experienced. Those three guys liked looking for unexploded bombs to throw themselves onto, just for the customer. They were like pigs in shit, and they slept on beanbags underneath their desks. It was in their DNA to serve. It was their mentality. These guys used to work for other people, but in organisations that didn't care about customer service. With Peer 1, they become legends.

Larry accomplished another epic feat after a cata-strophic tornado hit Southeast Asia and the resultant increase in donations toppled the site of a large UK aid agency. The agency could have potentially lost millions of pounds, which would have limited their ability to help people affected by the disaster. We were able to address hardware issues in the data centre, but the aid agency used third-party software for their website, and its team needed to make some changes before everything was totally fixed. They needed time and someone else needed to finalise the configura-tions at 2 am, because that was the time when the site received its lowest traffic volume.

Larry stepped in and coordinated with the tech team from third party. 'I'm the technical account manager for the aid agency,' he said. 'Train me on what I need to do at two o'clock in the morning. I'll get up at home at 1 am, have a cup of tea, log in at 2 am, and make the changes.'

That is how myths are made, with Larry becoming a legendary figure in the organisation. And knowing and sharing his story spurs other people to do greater feats.

Gather feedback and assess customer sentiment at the right moments

I was running a CRM consultancy that worked with a financial institution whose customers had a term policy that they then needed to reinvest. Using data analysis, we discovered a nugget of wisdom that I've been applying ever since. Here it goes: if you look at a client who's on a twelve-month contract, you could ask them if they're going to renew. And they might say 'yes' or 'no', but customers generally don't want to upset you. They think to themselves, 'Why would I want to have this difficult conversation if I don't need to?' So they just go, 'Yeah, of course we are.'

But what we found in the data was that if you can sell them something *else* six months before the renewal – it doesn't matter what it is – and they buy, they tend to renew the main contract. The very act of buying something from you gives an insight into their mental state.

More importantly, you gain visibility into which customers are likely to renew and which are likely to exit as soon as their term ends. You gain time to proactively perform either reinforcement techniques to drive loyalty or remedial measures to prevent attrition.

Don't forget to ask for referrals

You shouldn't get NPS at contract signing, when the customer is just registering with you. But getting referrals is another thing. The signatory has just ridden the emotional roller coaster of making a buying decision. They're excited about having done it and think they're smart for reaching this point. Positivity is in the air and everyone is on an emotional high. Now is a great time to ask for a referral.

Many people miss this trick. Unless you have a superb, flawless product or service, asking a customer who has been with you for a while might not lead to a favourable outcome. But asking right at the beginning, when the slate is clean, you have a far better chance of getting a referral or two.

This is where many people get it wrong: they think they have to deliver before asking for a referral. Wrong. You can go for the ask at exactly the moment when the purchase decision has been made.

In addition to referrals, this is an opportune moment to probe the customer for deeper insights about your product or service. For example, ask this:

Where did we nearly lose you?

More likely than not, you'll get an honest answer. That's because they want you to be better, now that they depend on your continued success. By making a purchase, they are also investing in you. They have an emotional connection with you.

Most companies ask for feedback from people who didn't buy, which is not a bad thing. Learning from people who rejected your product or service can lead to improvements in it. There could be a million reasons why a customer didn't buy, and you'll likely never be able to fix all of them, but you won't know if you don't ask.

Sell NPS with a story

To make your people love NPS, don't explain it to them. *Tell a story.*

That is how our client, David Tudehope, introduced NPS to his executive team. As the CEO of Macquarie Telecom Group, David understood that businesses operate in a world that makes decisions based on feelings, where only powerful stories can stir up the right emotions for motivating people or changing organisational culture.

And so David didn't harp on about the technical details when he communicated the importance of NPS to his team, which was a telco in Australia's highly competitive and saturated market.

Here's how one of his stories went.

A man called up the Macquarie help desk and said, 'Look, this is terrible. My wife's going abroad, and she hasn't set the phone up for international roaming. That's going to cost us a fortune.'

The woman on the service desk replied, 'That's not a problem, sir. Where's your wife? Can we meet her at the airport gate?'

The help desk specialist then picked a phone from stock, placed a SIM card in it, and registered it on the system. Next, she then took a taxi to the airport, and gave the caller's wife exactly what she needed to perk up her journey: a courtesy phone, all primed and ready for global roaming.

Happiness unfolded.

The best part of the story for me is that the caller wasn't a customer of Macquarie Telecom's mobile service.

Such stories differentiate Macquarie from other players in the market. The company's sustained focus on customer experience enables it to achieve the highest NPS in the industry (+76 for the 2022 financial year). Last year it won double gold, with Macquarie awarded Best Customer Experience and David picking up CEO of the Year.

At the onset, Macquarie Telecom wanted to be like Nordstrom, another brand that has attained legendary status when it comes to customer service and loyalty. One popular, crazy and oft-cited story recounts how the US-based store chain refunded a customer for an item (tyre snow chains) that wasn't even being sold from its shelves. The irate customer apparently

MIND YOUR F**KING BUSINESS

mistook the store for the tyre shop that previously operated in the building. Nonetheless, the Nordstrom salesman gave him a $25 refund, thanked him and invited him to come back.

Some say this story is true (including founder John Nordstrom) but others say it is apocryphal. In any case, the business lesson in this story, as well as the one featuring Macquarie Telecom, shines for everyone to see: *empower your employees to do the right thing, especially in situations that involve customers.* The reason is simple: it takes a legacy of exceptional customer service to become a great brand. Such legacy feeds on legendary, almost mythical stories about staff going above and beyond what's expected. These stories are told and retold during inductions, anniversaries and other corporate milestones to inspire people to do the right thing for customers, assuaging any fears that the cost or profitability of their individual action will be questioned.[25]

Summary

- Customer service is everything. Seek feedback from your customers to continuously improve – and remember, negative feedback is of far more value to you than positive reviews as it tells you where you're going wrong.

- Never ignore customer churn. It is more cost-effective to work on customer retention than customer generation.

- One key question in your feedback surveys makes all the difference: 'How likely are you to recommend our product or service?' This is essential to your Net Promoter Score (NPS), which is vital for corporate success. If you don't have an NPS strategy, adopt one.

- Hire customer-facing experts into your customer-facing team. Recruit from the hospitality and retail sectors. Don't expect your IT experts to be customer service experts.

- Talk to your customers. Find out what they want and give them it. Hear them when they present their problems to you. Say sorry when you f**k up.

- Celebrate your best customer-service providers and tell their story – the best examples will become legendary and create a legacy for your company for years to come.

3
Rethinking Your Talent Acquisition Strategy

The war for talent is fake news. The truest thing about it are the expletives you hear when clueless organisations, managers, and recruiters go ballistic over a non-problem they fear would unravel the sustainability of their business. And that's not the worst of it. The so-called 'talent war' is a corporate bogeyman they themselves help create.

When I talk to business leaders about recruitment and the job market, many repeat the lies and inaccuracies they hear in echo chambers that want them to think human talent is becoming rarer in a population of billions and in a landscape where access to knowledge is unprecedented. So much so that companies allegedly need to fight one another tooth and nail over a scarce number of skilled professionals worthy to join the workplace.

Surprisingly, neither these companies nor the people who run them actually engage in full-blown corporate wars over human talent. At best, they're acting like armchair generals – people who think they're HR experts but have no actual experience identifying and developing talented employees. Yet because the 'war for talent' catchphrase makes people appear knowledgeable about modern business, it gets bandied about, quite often casually mentioned in passing.

Making matters worse, many employers suck at finding, acquiring, and retaining talent, then wrongly project their own inadequacies and fears to the job market in general. Instead of acknowledging and addressing the gaps in their talent acquisition apparatus, organisations unconsciously deflect the blame to other factors: 'We can't hire good people because there's a war for talent.' To be blunt, that's the language of victims. Saying such things is the closest people get to the imaginary battlefield. It's also why the loaded term 'war for talent' remains a sticky part of corporate jargon.

How the talent war delusion creeps into a company

Organisations tend to hope that truly amazing candidates will ring them up and apply to join their payroll. But when I ask business leaders how often this fantasy happens in real life, the answer is always

'Never.' Allegedly, such an occurrence is like winning the lottery in the UK, the odds of which clocks in at around one in 14 million. Except the chances of most companies getting a call from a top-tier candidate might even be lower than hitting the jackpot or being struck by lightning. As a result, people choose not to buy tickets at all nor to play the recruitment game in earnest.

Fortunately, warmongers don't get the last laugh. Some companies succeed at attracting awesome people. Organisations that have cracked the code to talent acquisition have absolutely no problem finding and hiring top talent. These companies consistently draw in competent, creative and highly motivated professionals who generate tremendous value for their business.

While such talent magnets appear to have an unlimited pipeline of highly skilled professionals, everybody else thinks a war over talent scarcity is raging. These misinformed employers tend to blame other people, almost always pointing the finger at competitors for rigging the game by paying ludicrous salaries to high performers: 'I can't hire anybody because my competitors offer insane amounts of money.' (By the way, did you notice how that previous sentence is phrased from a victim perspective?)

Embracing the victim mindset makes it easier to justify being average. It diminishes a company's accountability for not trying to find and hire the right talent for their teams. Because they think it's not their fault that they can't attract good people, they get comfortable at hiring professionals with mediocre skills, character and vision.

This mental model perpetuates a cycle of mediocrity. And it doesn't take much to predict how the future would pan out for a company run by such people. Once a business is populated with sub-par employees, a common thought pattern emerges: 'Well, there's no point in getting rid of them because I couldn't get anyone better. Anyway, it's better to have them than to have no one on the team at all.'

When I suspect that a company I'm consulting with depends too much on mediocre staff, I waste no time reaching out and speaking with the CEO. We'll then have a conversation where I'll pop a key question about the quality of their people.

For many of my past clients, A-players – awesome employees, top-performing employees, etc – rarely accounted for more than 35% of the workforce at the outset. Their problems would have been a freak accident otherwise. Making things worse, most businesses suffer from a corporate equivalent of the Dunning–Kruger effect: they think they are a lot better than they truly are.[26]

When I work with companies like this, my role as a change agent kicks in, and I wear my growth hacker's hat. I'll make the CEO take the hard first steps towards transformation, which are:

1. See the true situation of the human aspects of the business.

2. Realise the imperative to change.

So with due empathy but in brutal honesty, a typical conversation would go like this:

>**Me:** What proportion of your staff do you recognise as A-players?

>**CEO:** Oh, I don't know. Maybe 50%?

>**Me:** You're deluded. Your A-players are my B-players. And your Bs wouldn't even make it to any of my teams.

The ABCs of talent acquisition

A business is only as good as the people in it. To truly transform a company, you need to focus on its human assets, starting from the leadership team down to the last staffer. As research consistently shows, nothing else impacts business success as much as human talent.[27] Which means the more top performers a company employs, the better it becomes at achieving targets, beating competitors, and driving growth.

But how exactly do you measure top performance or define A-players?

One excellent framework for classifying your workforce is the Topgrading system, which was introduced by renowned management psychologist Bradford D Smart.[28] Developed as a reliable tool for recruiting and developing talent, Topgrading is also a simple way of categorising all the people in an organisation based on their performance. The framework uses the categories A, B, and C as a reference for making specific HR-related decisions and to support talent management in general.

Intuitively, category A describes top performers (A-players), while B refers to generally reliable and competent workers (B-players), and C applies to underperforming employees (C-players). Ideally, most A-players go up the ranks and assume leadership positions. B-players are coached to eventually become A-players. C-players are further sorted into those who are retained for the possibility that they may yet improve and those who are advised to leave the company.

Topgrading and other talent management frameworks share the same objective: to help organisations achieve their desired business outcomes by making sense of and improving the quality of their human assets. When I speak with executives or give workshops, I often highlight this concept by asking questions like:

'What's the best team you've ever been in?' or, 'Which characteristics differentiate your best team players from the rest?'

I get several common responses when business leaders describe their best employee or ideal team:

- 'Oh, they're amazing and move fast.'

- 'Well, they're constantly doing the things I didn't ask them to do. They have this ability to just get on and do stuff.'

- 'When I delegate a task, they go and do it. They rarely need to be checked or managed.'

- 'They're self-motivated and work hard.'

- 'Everybody loves them. I never get complaints about them.'

I then raise a couple of follow-up questions and brace myself for the sad, predictable punchline.

> **Me:** Okay, so how many of these A-players do you have in your organisation?

> **CEO:** Three.

> **Me:** How many total people do you have?

> **CEO:** Seventy.

The frequency with which I have this type of conversation often makes me wonder WTF is wrong with the world. These companies employ a handful of A-players who are amazing. Many of the business leaders I talk with know full well the huge difference top-tier talent can deliver. So why do they still make half-hearted forays into the job market looking for – and taking in – people who aren't as good? And why do they even seem surprised when they're not meeting targets? But as usual, companies with chronically underperforming staff would rather play their 'war for talent' card, blaming everyone and everything else except themselves, when they sorely need to take a long, hard look in the mirror.

Fortunately, the cure for this corporate malady can be as simple as fine-tuning your talent management process. The trouble is, when I ask companies to show me how they go about hiring new talent, they describe an ad hoc process involving a third-party recruiter. They give the dullest job description to the recruiter, who then interviews any desperate candidate who saw and responded to the job ad.

By the way, that's the good news. Some companies don't even have a f**king process.

When you just email a recruiter, throw things around hoping someone catches something, and accept any candidate the recruiter recommends, then what you get is a quality control problem. Left to itself, this insane process will eventually implode into an existential crisis for the company. So instead of a war for talent, what you get is something potentially far worse: an apocalypse of mediocrity.

Yes, talent recruitment requires a f**king process

Every great or aspiring-to-be-great business needs an amazing hiring process. But for a company to build an effective talent pipeline, it must have a strategic mindset towards recruitment. Think of it as managing a football team. If you were Alex Ferguson helming Manchester United and you'd just won the European Championship and the Premier League, would you hire a striker who is far less capable than the ones you already have just because he'll sign up for less money?

You simply wouldn't do that. Instead, you might say, 'I have a great team. But I can make it even better. Which performance gaps should I fill first? Which types of professionals can fill those gaps and improve results?'

In any competitive field, you never hire anybody who's worse than the people you've already got. Unfortunately, businesses tend to overlook the possibility that they could have been hiring mediocre professionals who have eroded some aspects of their overall performance. That's because many companies primarily depend on third-party recruiters to do the searching and hiring for them.

Businesses assume recruiters are working to the same recruitment targets and talent acquisition goals as they are. That is rarely the case. Yes, companies pay the recruiter to do something. But unless a company tailors the contract in their favour, the recruiter will always work for the recruiter.

Alternatively, you can run a job ad yourself and receive hundreds of CVs. This sounds daunting, but there are some steps you can go through that increase your chances of hiring great people. It's a ton of work, but who says going to war is easy? Bear in mind that you should take this route only if you have a dynamic HR function. While large enterprises commonly have excellent in-house talent management units, small and mid-sized companies opt to work with external consultants and recruiters instead.

Ordinarily, the recruiter will send you ten CVs for example and say, 'Look, these are the best people available.' Let me tell you something: no, they are not. Those are mostly people who don't have jobs at the moment, plus one or two currently employed but discontented applicants. Nonetheless, the recruiter will insist that those are the best candidates in the market, and that you should interview at least three and hire the last one standing.

That pretty much describes the recruiter's process, which usually only finds low-hanging candidates and rarely goes deeper in the labour market to search for high performers who currently hold jobs. Sometimes they might even tap into people they placed somewhere before, which tends to undermine and annoy their other clients. The fact is nothing prevents recruiters from doing so. Who knows, you might even experience the same treatment where another company poaches good people from your payroll with the help of the very same recruiter who got them there in the first place. This is not to paint the entire career recruitment industry in a bad light. Many recruiters adopt excellent practices and maintain high ethical standards. However, not everyone does.

Talent acquisition outcomes largely depend on how many companies are willing to own the process even as they collaborate with recruiters. But few companies opt to take the high ground and make a conscious decision to take ownership of their recruitment process.

The interview: How to evaluate and work with recruiters

Recruiters can be heaven-sent, but only if you know how to work with them. On the other hand, run-of-the-mill recruiters can set you off on a hellish journey. The key is to let recruiters help you gather candidates for a particular role and build a short list. But you (as the company) and your HR unit (if you have one) should define excellence for every role in the company and own the interview process, especially when it comes to executive leadership and other important roles. After all, only you know your business inside out, including which specific traits, skills and experiences are needed to optimise every role in your operations.

What I've discovered through many years of hiring is that most recruiters lack the insight and incentive to conduct meaningful interviews. While it might be an element in their general process, in-depth interviews of shortlisted candidates don't always count as a core function in many recruitment agencies. Some recruiters conduct shitty, rushed interviews as a tick-box exercise so they can proceed to screen the next candidate.

But for organisations concerned with results and ROI, applicant interviews play a crucial part. Bad hires mean bad investments, wasted money and lost time. Reinforced by experts and proper tools – assessment tools or role-specific tests – conducting your own interviews is an effective way to manage risks and optimise gains when it comes to talent acquisition.

To reiterate, owning the interview process doesn't mean going about it yourself unaided. I rarely meet businesspeople who have been trained thoroughly enough to conduct interviews. Think of it this way:

if you're a car owner and your vehicle breaks down, you might try to fix it yourself if you have some rudimentary DIY knowledge. But it's a lot better to seek assistance from an expert mechanic. In the same way, top-notch recruiters, management consultants and executive search agencies have the training and resources required to get the most out of job interviews. Yet to achieve optimal outcomes, you also need to align their process to your unique needs and take charge when they run the interviews.

Unfortunately, many businesses opt to work with run-of-the-mill recruiters or do the interviews themselves. In both cases, this often leads to talent acquisition disasters. These, in turn, lead to some sort of post-decision cognitive dissonance: 'Well, we couldn't hire good people because there weren't any good people to hire.' You won't hear companies saying the likelier truth in the matter: 'We couldn't hire good people because we're shit at finding them.'

Tools and tactics for talent hunting

The job market may not be a war zone, but it surely is a wilderness. You need the proper equipment and the right tactics to survive and come out on top. Let's take a look at some of the most effective tools and techniques that I have used over the years when leading organisations to achieve high performance.

Topgrading methodology

Previously mentioned in this chapter, Topgrading is a hiring and performance assessment framework used by many world-class organisations, such as Barclays, Sun Life, Shell Oil, and Microsoft. This system uses extensive interviews, performance scorecards and job history to categorise employees into A-, B- and C-players. A-players are star performers, B-players are adequately competent, and C-players are under-achievers, the worst of whom are subsequently asked to leave the company.

Remember:

- Topgrading is *not* stack ranking.

- An A-player can be defined as a professional belonging to the top 10% of available talent in a given location for a given job on a given salary. They're not more expensive, but they can generate ten times more value than their lower-rated peers.

- Aiming to build a workforce composed overwhelmingly (around 90%) by A-players is not a ludicrous goal.

- Given advances in communications technology and business networks, you can source A-players from more favourable near-shore or off-shore locations, if sourcing them in your actual location is too difficult.

Gallup's CliftonStrengths assessment test

Gallup CliftonStrengths (formerly StrengthsFinder) is a talent management tool designed to classify employees based on their core personal strengths. Developed by analytics and advisory firm Gallup Inc., this personal assessment test outlines employee character attributes that are further defined by four domains: executing, influencing, relationship building, and strategic thinking.[29]

Using this popular assessment test is a win–win for all parties, regardless of whether the company will ultimately hire the applicant. That's because both the employer and the candidate will gain useful insights about their individual strengths. Applicants who have not made the cut will still leave the process with something of value to them.

Use this test and the interview process in conjunction with a warm and open attitude towards all applicants. When you do this, everyone applying wants to get hired by the company, they have a positive attitude about you as an employer, and they will gladly refer their friends to apply to the company too – whether they get hired or not. This has happened so frequently in my experience that it would be criminal of me not to mention it.

Job analysis development tool

I've developed a job analysis tool based on Brad Smart's Topgrading framework. I commonly share this tool with clients as a mechanism for defining a role, prioritising specific tasks related to the role, and scoring the performance of the person who successfully gets appointed. The tool follows a simple mantra: for whatever role you want to fill, you have to start with the end in mind.

For example, how will you assess whether your new hire has performed well after one year of assuming the role? Obviously, you'll need to define the major tasks and activities related to the role as well as the relevant metrics and KPIs, which define a certain number or threshold as the indicator of success. Starting with the end in mind in this case, you would list three to five things that will be used to evaluate whether the employee has been excellent or not. What are the things you want their specific role to accomplish? How will you measure their performance?

I ask my clients to create a simple job analysis meeting table/spreadsheet with the following five columns:

- **Activities/Tasks:** Start by defining the activities involved in the role.

- **Time:** This refers to how long the activity/task takes. If a task takes less than 5% of the role's time, you can scratch it out.

- **Impact:** What is the effect of the activity/tasks – do they have high, medium or low impact on the business?

- **Frequency:** Is the task performed daily, weekly, monthly or annually? If the frequency is annual, only keep it on your list if the task is also high impact.

- **Measurement:** Here, you'll add in the KPIs.

During a meeting with a new potential employee, use your job analysis meeting table/spreadsheet to jot down pertinent information about them.

Job analysis development example

Activity (tasks)	Time (= 5%)	Impact (H/M/L)	Frequency (D/W/M/A)	Measurement (KPI)
Reduce churn	✓	H	D	1.3% per month
Grow client base	✓	H	D	+3% gross per month
Develop talent of support team	✓	H	D	70% A-players

How to write amazing job ads

Your first contact with top-tier talent can occur via a job ad. But beware: if A-players see a shitty job ad, you'll scare them off.

Unfortunately, shitty ads are almost always what they'll see. Just take a look at all the job ads on career search platforms online. You'll find the same ad template making the rounds: boast (or lie) about how great your company is, mention a boring and unrealistic litany of required skills for the role, and end with a list of unremarkable compensation offers and benefits.

When a job ad talks largely about how great the employer is, it treads the path of narcissistic irrelevance. In contrast, amazing job descriptions are always applicant-centric. I learned this via an excellent book by Mark Murphy. Aside from giving the valuable insight of placing a high premium on behaviour and self-motivation, Murphy's book, *Hiring for Attitude: A revolutionary approach to recruiting and selecting people with both tremendous skills and superb attitude*, also features an excellent section on how to write awesome job ads.[30]

To buck the trend and genuinely connect with world-class talent, speak to their specific frustrations, aspirations and goals. You can ask your A-players what makes their jobs at your company less frustrating and which aspects support their short-term and long-term goals. Highlight those in your ad instead of bragging about your company.

Take a look at these sample punchy messages you could use in your ads, which speak directly to the candidate:

- You're amazing at sales, and you hit your numbers pretty much all the time. But when was the last time you learned something new from your manager?

- You're a marketing professional, but you prefer using spreadsheet software than a colour palette. Wonderful! You'll have fun in our team as director of demand generation.

- The challenge of creating elegant codes excites you. The shrill voice of your bossy team lead doesn't. Care to check out our diverse and dynamic group of software developers? Oh, and by the way, nobody will shout at you.

Timing the interview

The final thing to consider is to make sure that the interview process moves fast – as soon as a potential A-player signals that he or she is interested in the role. Don't let a week pass by without creating a major touchpoint. Otherwise, the candidate might forget about your ad or could have learned how to handle the stress at their current employer. If a currently employed candidate had a good or promising week at their employer, you can bid the hiring opportunity goodbye.

A good rule of thumb is, ideally, you'll take the candidate from interest to offer in a single week. Not easy, but achievable.

Four touchpoints in the interview stage

I recommend four touchpoints when it comes to orchestrating job interviews and ensuring their success:

Phone interview with HR

Conduct this touchpoint with at least two interviewers. Ensure that it involves somebody from HR who is good at interviewing and the leader of the unit the candidate is applying for. A core function of the team lead (the de facto hiring manager) in this scenario is to clarify the role and sell the job to the candidate, with the aim of building an emotional connection.

Having at least two interviewers enables your company to ask all the right questions without affecting its ability to evaluate answers in real time. It also shores up the decision on whether to take the process to the next phase by requiring a green light from both interviewers – if one gives a thumbs down, then it's over.

A picture paints a thousand words

Go beyond the candidate's CV by asking them to draw something that motivates or inspires them. Use paper and a set of coloured pens or pencils. Ideally, this touchpoint should give a glimpse into their personalities, thought processes and emotional state. For this stage, forget the CV and just focus on the picture for about half an hour. It's amazing what it will reveal. Once, an applicant gave herself away as a chronic narcissist by drawing three pictures of herself all in red, then talking about me, me, me the whole time. She did not get the job. On the other hand, you'll find people drawing sunshine, blue skies and stick figures going up a mountain. You'll have deep conversations about their passions, family and personal aspirations, all of which builds trust and creates the all-important emotional connection that might be missing with their present employer.

Panel presentation

Require shortlisted candidates to do a simple presentation (no need to be fancy) about why working for the company is a good move and why the company should hire them. This touchpoint is not about presentation skills. It's about the applicant's willingness to go the extra mile (preparing the presentation the night before the interview) and about selling the company and the role to themselves. This will help you separate the wheat from the chaff and further shorten the list to only candidates who are hungry for the role and who have a fundamental understanding of its expectations and functions.

Meet the team

Have the candidates meet, work and collaborate with the relevant team in some form or another. Wherever legal, have some type of trial period or part-time contract, whereby the candidate as well as the team can evaluate job and culture fit before proceeding to formal employment. Make sure the candidate interacts only with A-players from the team. Scrap this touchpoint if all you have are B-players, especially when you are trying to hire top-tier talent.

Onboarding and talent development

Giving employees memorable, emotional and positive experiences is one of the most impactful methods for building trust, improving retention rates and driving high performance. Consider these two scenarios describing a new hire's first day on the job:

Scenario A: Doug arrives at the office and finds that he doesn't have a desk – not even a dedicated chair, phone or laptop. Doug's new boss is too busy to show him around, instead telling Doug to shadow other colleagues until he learns the ropes.

Scenario B: Sally receives a welcome card via snail mail the weekend before her first day. When she arrives at the office, the smiling CEO leads her to a large meeting room, where everyone on the team gives her a warm greeting. Later, she's shown to her desk and receives clear guidance about what she'll be up to for her first few days.

Whose experience will likely drive them towards high performance? Put it this way, if I were Doug, I'd be getting my CV right back out there. To be sure, habits and discipline serve as key performance drivers, but don't make the mistake of overlooking the importance of your employees' positive emotions.

When it comes to talent development for your new and existing employees, you can use the tools you have already at hand. Companies that use Topgrading as a framework can extend its principles to talent development. By using an employee's past performance and classification as a benchmark, you can set new (but reasonable) targets for employees to retain, if they were an A-player, or improve, if they were B-players or C-players. This ensures continuous skills and performance improvement over time.

But what do you do with C-players who are unable or unwilling to improve themselves? The short answer is that it's quite possible that you'll have to remove them from your organisation. First, though, there are a few things you can try first, to ensure you're removing the right people. If they aren't a cultural fit, skip right to the exit. If they are a cultural fit, first try:

- Changing their manager

- Narrowing the focus of their role

- Giving them some specific training

In ninety days, reassess by asking yourself whether they now have the potential to be A-players and whether you would enthusiastically rehire them. If you answer either of these with a 'no', then you have your answer.

Firing people is never easy. But the alternative – keeping employees who are either low performing, or who are high performing yet delivering their results at the expense of others on their team (toxic A-players) – will be detrimental to you, your team and your company.

When dealing with a poor performer, including when terminating their employment, always be transparent and honest. Also, make sure you involve HR so that everyone follows the right processes.

Summary

- There is no 'war for talent'. There are good people out there, and it's your job to find them, interview them and hire them.

- Use Topgrading to find out who your A-players are. Hire more of these people. Identify your B-players and C-players. If they can't be transformed into A-players, be prepared to let them go.

- A talent-management process is a requirement, not an option. If you're going to use recruitment agencies as part of your process, make them work for you. Tell them who you want and get them to find the best candidates, not just anyone.

- If you're handling recruitment yourself, you've got to put in the work. Know who you're targeting, write a killer job ad, and use a rapid hiring process with character analysis and four interview stages to get the best people into your company.

- The onboarding process is just as important as the interview process. If you want your new recruit to turn up on day two (and three, four, five, etc), give them a great experience on day one.

4
Employer Brand: Always Be Recruiting

When it comes to attracting talent, some companies seem to have all the luck. Google, for example, receives a tsunami of applications (around 50,000 CVs per week),[31] many of them from top-tier professionals and graduates. While other organisations struggle to recruit and retain top talent, top brands get the sweetest slice of the pie – brands such as Salesforce, Microsoft, Abcam, Google, and Softcat in the UK, and in the US, brands like Bain & Company, Nvidia, In-N-Out Burger, HubSpot, and McKinsey & Company.

But luck has nothing to do with it. The secret is in plain sight for all to see: it takes the right kind of reputation to catch a jobseeker's interest and make them want to join your company. Which of course leads to the next inconvenient truth: it takes hard f**king work to build a culture that drives and sustains a compelling employer brand.

This is probably why many organisations don't even bother to take the next step, choosing instead the far easier path of blaming all their HR woes on the so-called war for talent. Unfortunately, this option is self-destructive and merely leads to lower levels of employee satisfaction, worker engagement, and profitability.

Meanwhile, experience and evidence have demonstrated that higher worker satisfaction leads to better retention rates and stock performance. Ultimately, having a great culture impacts financial results.[32] This is partly because happy employees just can't keep the merriment to themselves and will most likely share their good vibes with customers.[33] And as every business owner knows, the happier your customers are, the cheerier your income statements become.

So here's the rub. How in the world will customers love your company if your staff don't?

Customer satisfaction: Love starts at home

People say that their employees are the most important thing in their business. After all, the product they sell is just a commodity, and if it carries the same price as those of their competitors, then customer service becomes the main differentiator. At the end of the day, customer service largely depends on the quality of frontline talent.

While businesses acknowledge all of this, their actions contradict their words. Instead of driving aggressive talent recruitment strategies, most companies rarely do anything special to attract the best people onto their payroll. But as workplace surveys and studies confirm, highly engaged workers help drive customer satisfaction.[34] Engaged employees deliver the effort needed to keep customers satisfied, achieve better financial results, drive innovation, and significantly outperform competitors.[35]

Every business treats customer satisfaction as a crucial component of their strategy because unhappy customers lead to churn, which in turn erodes revenue. This sad trajectory can be reversed by improving employee engagement. Engaged workers willingly go the extra mile because they share a strong connection with the company and its goals. For this reason, business owners, managers and leaders should go beyond job descriptions to really understand what motivates their people. It's equally important to ask the difficult questions. Do your employees love working for your business? Only when you find this to be true will you have a strong brand as an employer.

Why is that important? If you have a strong brand, professionals will do everything they can to join your company – even when you're not actively recruiting.

How to build a compelling brand

Google your company name. Then click 'Images'. What do you see?

On your screen are the same visuals prospective employees will see about your company. Do the images convey healthy doses of fun and passion? Would they inspire potential workers to want to achieve more than they think they could? Or are the images just stock photos of generic and inauthentic corporate scenes that will more likely repel than attract A-players?

Of course, what people see on Google Images doesn't show the complete picture of your brand. But it's a start, and first impressions linger.

Attract the right people

Consider a top-tier professional suffering from Sunday Night Fear (a workplace-related condition characterised by high anxiety levels on Sunday in fearful anticipation of another week of soul-sapping work). As a business owner, manager or team leader, you'd want to reach out to this person: a competent, currently employed professional who is unhappy about their employer. Frustrated A-players like them number more than you think they do. In fact, around half of workers in the legal, electronics, and tourism industries suffer from Sunday Night Fear.[36] Meanwhile, around 67% of media practitioners and 44% of finance professionals dread Mondays.[37]

While stressed out, some of these professionals have the skills, experience, and attitude that can make a difference in your business. They're a surer bet than the pool of unemployed people who are actively looking for jobs, which is more likely to have a higher proportion of B- or C-players among its number.

The three major types of professionals that make up the talent market are as follows:

1. The unemployed. You'll have to spend time separating the wheat from the chaff in this segment. Most recruiters target this demographic, so be smart when working with talent agencies and third-party recruiters.

2. Decent professionals who suffer from Sunday Night Fear. These are the ones you want. Focus on these workers.

3. Excellent employees who like where they work and aren't looking for a new employer. While these professionals most likely work for your competitors, you should still aim to get them on

your team. But the only way you can hire them is to know what motivates them other than money, so take every opportunity to talk with them about what drives them and makes them tick.

Polish your public image

Now you know who you want to attract, how do you connect with them? Imagine this common scenario. Driven by anxiety over the new work week ahead, an A-player sits on the couch, twiddles a tablet and looks for whatever can calm their nerves or keep their attention. Perhaps they're thinking, 'F**k me, I'll be repeating the same crappy experience tomorrow. There must be a better job than this shit.' Hoping they can flee their current job, they visit job listings or the websites of their favourite brands. What would they find if one of these was yours?

Just as importantly, what would they discover on industry reports, such as those that rank the companies in that sector? What about career sites that allow employees to rate or review their employers? Best Companies, for example, partners with *The Sunday Times* to rank the top UK employers in many key categories and sectors.[38] On the other side of the Atlantic, *Fortune* collaborates with Great Place to Work to publish their annual *100 Best Companies to Work For* report.[39]

It would be awesome if your company features in either list. But if that's not the case, you can still polish your brand on career-focused sites that feature employer profiles. Glassdoor is a good place to start. This site encourages workers to review current and former employers, their CEOs and the pros and cons of joining. Based on this feedback and other data, Glassdoor annually publishes its popular *Best Places To Work: Employees' Choice* report.[40] So even if your company doesn't make it to the Top 100 list, jobseekers can still read the reviews, ratings and recommendations of your current and former employees.

Is your brand strong enough to set off a positive reaction? Being recommended by at least 80% of reviewers would constitute a decent brand. The best have a CEO approval rating of above 90%. Aim for an overall score of at least 4.0 out of 5; 4.2 or higher would put you in the top 50 companies in the UK. Anything below 4.0 generally describes you as a less than amazing employer on Glassdoor.

Does your company make the cut? Do you rank better than your competitors? If not, you can expect top-tier jobseekers to prioritise other employers, leaving you with a pool of mediocre candidates.

Keep your people happy

To attract the right candidate, you need to clarify what it takes to be the best employee in your organisation. Then you need to ask yourself, 'Why in the world would this person want to join my company?'

Start by identifying the proportion of top performers in your payroll, using talent management tools such as the ones we looked at in Chapter Three. If you find that you have very few quality performers in your team, chances are that most A-players in your industry work for better-leveraged competitors. What would it take for these top-notch professionals to leave their current employers and work for your business?

That's right, an awesome employer reputation.

Business owners, HR managers and team leaders need to make an honest self-assessment as to how other people view their company. If you get everything right, you don't even have to advertise for a vacant job. Without being nudged, professionals will send you their applications – as long as your brand meets their expectations and your culture matches their aspirations. One recruitment company that I worked with, La Foss Associates, has consistently ranked top in listings of UK recruiters for ten years. Not surprisingly, they have zero recruitment challenges. Hordes of candidates send in their CVs every year.

If you have problems finding and hiring great people, you should check out how the best competitors in your industry cope with their recruitment. Explore review sites, company rankings and awards programmes to find out which recruitment techniques and cultural realignment strategies work and which don't.

Benefits can also be key to attracting the right people. Benefits cost less to offer employees than large salary increases and are often a proxy for the culture of an organisation. At Peer 1 we took the decision to make sure our salaries were midmarket, adding a regular review to make sure we kept pace with the market. To enable us to attract talent in all twenty-two of our locations, in multiple countries, where we were hiring staff, we offered what we considered to be world-class benefits. We had a pool table, foosball tables, darts, a slide in the office, pitch and putt minigolf, and a pub. We also offered flexible working hours, enhanced paternity leave, childcare vouchers, a cycle to work scheme, death in service and medical benefits. To further enhance our offering, we looked at the companies we admired, as well as those listed in 'best place to work' lists, and added comparable benefits that we felt made sense as part of our package. Some were free to all staff, like ice creams in the freezer all summer; others, such as help with childcare costs, were available through a salary sacrifice scheme. Employees could spend up to 5% of their salary on benefits before they then incurred any other costs.

I have recently had clients remove their requirement for new employees to serve any probationary period. Their job adverts clearly say, 'NO PROBATION'. This has cost them nothing, doesn't stop them removing poor-performing new hires and sends a strong message about their culture.

Whatever approach you choose, it is essential to treat your people with respect. Appreciate their value and give the recognition they deserve each time their work meets your standards of excellence. Not only is this the right thing to do, it's also a safe way to trigger a dopamine rush, which helps drive employee engagement,[41] which in turn positively impacts business performance.

This is why the fourth question in the popular Gallup Q^{12} Employee Engagement Survey[42] goes something like this: 'In the last seven days, have you received recognition or praise for doing good work?' While this question primarily assesses the quality of managers, it also reflects the company environment, culture and brand.

Unfortunately, many companies practise the so-called Mushroom Principle instead, which is basically keeping staff in the dark and feeding them shit. I remember working for a UK business that at the time was Britain's best managed company. In one of their warehouses, there was a poster on the wall that said, *'Doing a good job around here is like pissing yourself in a dark suit. It gives you a warm feeling, but nobody notices.'*

Think about how undermining that poster is. The company had an amazing public image, but nobody tore down that poster because what it said was true. When you're not communicating with staff, when you're not recognising their discretionary effort to make your business awesome, then you're creating an environment that will only drive people away.

In my many years as a worker and business leader, there are two things staff rarely complain about:

1. Being overpraised for a job well done. Has anyone ever said to you, 'Can you please stop telling me I'm doing a great job?'

2. Getting too much feedback or 'over-communication' from their managers.

Bottom line: if you're not hearing either of the above complaints, then you need to praise or communicate with your people more.

Benching: Always be recruiting

It's undoubtedly challenging recruiting great people. Consider getting help from specialists. For example, one small London-based company helps organisations become great places to work. Run by a friend, Henry Stewart, Happy Ltd has been setting recruitment best practices for years.[43]

One remarkable practice the company implements is to 'bench' good candidates who, for some reason or another, don't end up coming on board. Benching is a common practice in sports where reserve players are seated on the sidelines in standby mode in case they're needed. Reportedly, Happy keeps a bench of 350 email addresses belonging to professionals they can send job ads to anytime and invite in for interviews. These professionals either apply for open jobs or refer other candidates who fit the roles. As a result, Happy generally finds, interviews and hires a competent professional for any role within a week or so.

In short, the message Happy gives out is this: 'If you'd like to work here, please stay in touch and enrol your email on our website. We'll reach out to you as soon as a job opens.' When the moment comes, the company delivers on its promise: 'Hey, we have a vacancy for a role. Would you like to apply?'

What Happy normally does is to build relationships and maintain strong connections with all the excellent professionals they come into contact with, including those outside their payroll. If it's just not the right time for Happy or the A-player to commit to an employment agreement, that doesn't mean the opportunity won't arise in the future, and since a touchpoint has already been established, nurturing the relationship moving forward serves as a strategic competitive advantage. In fact, the clients I work with who are scaling up pretty much always need to hire new talent, often in support of their sales efforts. Diligent businesses like these would benefit from sending callouts for competent salespeople even if they're not in actual hiring mode.

Benching also supports the oft-cited mantra that encapsulates the ABC of the sales world: Always Be Closing. Adopted in the field of talent acquisition, the slogan can also be thought of as Always Be Conscripting or Always Be Recruiting. This mindset is a crucial element in any long-term business strategy.

When I run companies or lead business units, I probably spend at least 20% of my time searching for top talent to hire. But if you ask many CEOs how much time they spend recruiting, their answers lack any real sense of urgency. 'I don't recruit anymore. The managers do it.' This is rather sad because in addition to augmenting your workforce, an Always Be Recruiting mindset ensures that you have the highest possible number of A-players in your team. You'd maintain a high-quality workforce by letting C-players go and replacing them with a new batch of actual and potential A-players.

Because you have already assessed the competencies of professionals on your employment bench, it's much easier to tap that existing shortlist than to scramble to create an entirely new one when a vacancy suddenly arises. Relying purely on job ads when you need new staff forces you to search for rare performers in a pool of mediocre candidates.

When you do make a connection with A-players, seize every opportunity to fast-track the recruitment process. Don't wait for a CV if they have an updated

LinkedIn profile. Instead, say, 'Why don't you just send me your LinkedIn profile and a phone number, and we'll talk.' Keep in mind that professionals who experience Sunday Night Fear will be more likely to join your company if you can interview and onboard them within a week of making contact. That's because their emotional state and sentiment about their current employment might improve over the next few days. When that happens, they have a stronger reason to stay put and a weaker incentive to join your company.

Recall and implement the four touchpoints cited in Chapter Three. Don't leave everything to a third-party recruiter. And another thing – when I engage new clients, I deliberately steer the conversation towards the quality of leadership. Excellence should always start from the top down, because A-players will always hire A-players, while B-players tend to hire from the B- and C- categories. More importantly, A-players will eventually feel bitter about working for B-level leaders down the road. This can lead to a sad and costly exodus of top talent from your company to your competitors.

CEOs should look at their leadership and ask the hard question: 'Are all of these people *really* A-players?' Sometimes, and with stronger impact, I raise the question myself to the CEO during leadership meetings where everyone in the team can hear. The courageous leaders who have been having difficult conversations with their team have no problem calling out the A, B and C grades of their team.

Laws of attraction and repulsion

Recruiting is hard, tedious work. That's why employers are more than willing to test whether a specific tool, approach or workaround would really improve their hiring process. And they're generally happy to adopt anything that accelerates or simplifies talent acquisition.

One approach that works for me is to use the hiring experience to quickly get rid of unsuitable candidates while motivating excellent ones to pursue their application. This attract–repel tactic expedites recruitment and makes it less painful, by dissuading inadequate candidates from applying at the outset. This can be done in several ways, but using customised job advertisements and web pages (for careers, company mission, core values, etc) is a good start.

For example, you can purposely design your job ads and careers page to resonate only with self-driven, results-focused professionals. For ads, make sure you use a scorecard to distil the role into its core expectations and activities. The scorecard concept should be applied for every role in your organisation, from sales support to CEO. When the messaging in your ads or web copy emphasises performance tracking and high standards of excellence, most mediocre workers won't even bother to send in an application. Based on your definition of an A-player, decline to interview applicants whose CVs don't meet the criteria.

If some underqualified applicants persist, then the interview/selection process should come as an uncomfortable experience for them to finally decide to discontinue their application. Remember, you don't need – and should not – use any method that disrespects people. Make the discomfort purely psychological, not personal, for example, where they sit there thinking, 'This company is serious about hard work and sterling results. Not a good place for slackers like me.'

You also have the nuclear option to decline someone on the spot. You can and should say no after the interview if you determine that, for whatever reason, a candidate has failed to meet the threshold. Doing this is kinder than letting the process continue only to cut it at a further point, where an applicant already harbours a strong expectation of being hired.

My experience looking for a job many years ago illustrates the attract–repel principle. During an interview, the employer said that around 10% of the bonus I'd earn would depend on being early for work, ie arriving before 9 am. At that time, I'd never been early for anything in my life, and the company wasn't somewhere I wanted to work. So I just dropped the entire thing. The idea of being early repelled my juvenile mindset. Of course, that has changed over the years. Now I obsess over punctuality.

Discouraging mediocre jobseekers from sending their applications shouldn't be limited to entry-level or mid-level positions – apply the approach for leadership positions, including C-suite roles. One way to do that is to set verifiable or measurable expectations (ie a scorecard) after a candidate has spent a year on the job. For example, if the leadership position involves sales targets or market expansion, then your job ads should state exactly what your targets are (eg 30% year-on-year profit growth, establishment of new retail outlets or offices in several cities, etc). When less-competent applicants get cold feet agonising over how they can orchestrate the expected results, they'll likely discontinue their application. 'I won't be able to deliver. Better look for another prospect.' And that leaves you with a shortlist of high performers.

Instead, we see job ads that say a certain company needs a college graduate with a minimum experience of three years. That's bullshit. If you do this, expect hundreds of applications to overwhelm your HR department, none of them properly matching the role and competence you have in mind. For every role, always go for CVs that emphasise relevant achievements using verifiable numbers and data. (Eg 'My sales team grew revenue by 40% over a six-month period.')

Retaining top talent

Hiring good people is one thing. Getting them to stay is another. Certainly, career development opportunities and pay structure impact employee satisfaction. But so do factors such as culture, sense of purpose, transparency, autonomy, recognition and communication. These latter factors tend to have more influence over worker engagement and retention.

Meanwhile, if an A-player is managed by and surrounded by people who aren't themselves A-players, they might simply pack their bags and go. Think about it. How would you feel if you did more of the heavy lifting than your colleagues, *and* you were paid the same or even less than others on your team? There are few things more demotivating than that. You might stay with the company a while, but seeking an exit would be almost inevitable.

Even 'minor' issues such as commuting have been found to significantly affect the mental health, well-being, and attrition rates of employees in the UK.[44] Evidence indicates that if your commute is more than forty-five minutes long, you'll likely change jobs at some point just to get more time back, not money. For this reason, I only consider applicants who live within forty-five minutes of the office. I always aim to build a team with high engagement levels, and that's nearly impossible to do with professionals who spend hours commuting every day. They simply will deliver less discretionary effort, which is the currency for excellence and innovation.

Because a company's financial performance depends on employee engagement and talent retention, business owners should build a sound strategy on how to keep their top-performing employees longer and to have more of them in the roster.

Design your brand around your A-players

When I sit down with clients, most of them would say that A-players account for 10% to 35% of their staff. I'd then advise that they need to reach 90%, because there's simply no business day when everything turns out to be ideal. Processes will have bottlenecks and individuals will have shitty days. What if your handful of A-players call in sick or go on holiday? Left with a team of average and below-average performers, you'll need an insane level of luck to make your business succeed.

Perhaps 90% is daunting to you, but I've worked for companies where A-players accounted for 70% of the total workforce. It is possible – and definitely challenging. One of my clients took twelve months of active recruiting to get to 50%, and they're on the way to achieving the 90% target.

This is another good opportunity to establish how to define your ideal employee. When I engage clients about this, they describe their best people in many ways, using phrases such as:

- 'He constantly surprises me with things that I didn't ask for.'

- 'Clients keep telling me that she's amazing.'

- 'I don't need to manage him.'

Imagine the achievements and performance level of a company whose workforce is composed of such employees. That's why your employer brand should treat this elite subset of professionals as your target audience. Your brand and culture should be designed and iterated to attract and retain these A-players, and to improve your B-players so that they become A-players. Also, this mindset should form part of your company's core values, purpose and overall strategy. As advances in technologies make remote work more feasible, extend your definition of A-players to include top talent from other locations, some of whom you can hire as long-term contractors.

To ensure that your workforce has a healthy proportion of A-players, you can adopt the attract–repel approach into your talent management strategy. At Rackspace, for example, the two words that summed up the essence of our company were: 'Fanatical Support'. We had the stated mission to be the world's best IT service business. Rackspace aimed to become and remain the 'Ritz Carlton of IT services'. Yet a good number of people who do IT support don't see customer service as their thing. The same issue popped up in Peer 1 (now Aptum Technologies). There was a guy who left a Linux system admin job to join our customer support team. But he soon quit, saying, 'I just hate talking to customers. I just want to deal with my computers again.'

In both cases, that infamous air of IT support arrogance became apparent, and we had to weed out people who didn't like to speak to customers. It made us realise that for the business to thrive and for the brand to be authentic, we had to discourage people who didn't like talking to people from applying for customer-facing jobs. We had to repel this type of professional, not only at the outset, but at any point in the process simply because their mindset did not fit our culture, brand or strategy.

Once the ideal candidate gets clearly defined at the hiring stage, you can implement the same tactic to the onboarding process. The critical element for this is the employee's scorecard (the job analysis development tool discussed in Chapter Three). Among other things, the scorecard shows a checklist of core (high-impact) activities a worker is expected to do, as well as everything they need to achieve in a given time frame. This will help you identify and develop A-players while screening out hires who aren't performing as well as expected. Ideally, you want a counterpoint to your 'hire fast' policy. That is, you also need a 'fire fast' policy to weed out poor performers and keep your team sharp by augmenting the number of A-players.

Summary

- Your employee brand affects everything – your hiring process, worker engagement and talent retention. The better your brand, the more A-players you keep on your payroll.

- Aim to have your brand included in popular industry rankings, particularly in 'Best Places to Work' reports. Work towards having strong scores and positive reviews on Glassdoor and other company review sites.

- Have as many A-players in your team as you can. Provide a unique recruitment experience (personal, creative and theatrical) that will make every candidate want to join your company even if they fail to make the cut in the end. For non-technical roles, hire more for attitude, less for skills. You can fix skill deficits with proper training.

- Implement the attract–repel tactic to weed out poor performers and increase the number of A-players in all your teams. Start with leadership, especially the C-suite. There is absolutely no room for B-players in that group. Leaders who are B-players will only drive A-players to exit.

- To measure how engaged your workers are, consider using the Gallup Q^{12} Employee Engagement Survey. This is a simple twelve-question survey that can help you gauge workforce satisfaction.

- Avoid the Mushroom Principle – never keep workers in the dark and feed them shit. Replace this culture with an environment of transparency, respect and robust communication.

- Treat everyone, including contractors, as human beings, not second-class citizens. Be known as an employer that adopts friendly policies towards traditionally marginalised worker demographics such as women who have recently given birth – generous maternity leave, flexible work arrangements, etc.

- Lastly, remember to recognise the value of talent. Never scrimp on praising a job done well.

5
F**k Annual Employee Appraisals, Embrace Weekly Check-ins

Do you want to know what annual appraisals are? They're twelve months of avoiding difficult conversations. Some companies perform annual appraisals so poorly that they should just stop doing them altogether. It can be more detrimental to do yearly evaluations than not to do them. Leaders ask the wrong questions of the wrong people. Clear objectives haven't been set, and not enough input from the employee is involved. An added problem is that people aren't as objective as they think they are. The following line from Marcus Buckingham's and Ashley Goodall's book, *Nine Lies About Work*, brilliantly captures this idea: 'Why is it a settled truth that your manager can reliably rate you on performance, when, on actual teams, none of us has ever met a team leader blessed with perfect objectivity?'[45] Deloitte called this the 'idiosyncratic rater effect', reporting that 'assessing someone's skills is subjective and says more about the rater rather than the ratee.'[46]

Rarely have leaders or managers been taught how to do annual appraisals, and when the time comes around to do them, they're usually unprepared and overworked. For instance, when a manager has to do ten appraisals in December, their workload has just doubled for that short month. That's a massive workload spike during an already busy season. Add to that the fact that they've had no training in appraisals, and they don't have much practice since this is an annual task. And managers are rarely entirely honest as it's hard to cram a year's worth of feedback into one meeting, and conversations may be too difficult to have at that point. So they grind through the appraisals sloppily, half-heartedly, and just want to get them over with.

But the core problem is that annual appraisals can't address an employee's concerns, problems, questions, strengths or weaknesses in real time. They can't teach the right lesson at the right time because it's delayed until the end of the year. Somehow, we've got it into our heads that it's better to have one big conversation at the end of the year than many little ones throughout the year. It's too late to fix, redirect or mentor someone after everything has already happened. People need honest, direct and inspiring feedback when the need arises.

Still not convinced? Think back to your childhood. Did your parents sit you down at the end of the year and teach you a few lessons, or did they teach you valuable lessons in the moment?

Real-time feedback is essential

Employees need to learn on the job, not after the job has been done. They need insights, suggestions, expertise and direction in the moment. What use is it months after the moment has passed? When was the last time you heard about a football coach talking to his players solely at the end of the year? He's hands-on before, during and after the match. The players need training during practice, direction during the game and feedback after the game is over. Yet companies are bent on annual employee appraisals that at best do nothing or, worse, cause significant problems.

Nobody plays a sport without knowing the rules, the boundaries or the score. Everybody needs to be clear about the game we're playing, how we win and what the score is in real-time. Who cares which team will be in the championship at the end of the year when you're not sure how well you're doing in the second game of the season? With an annual appraisal, you may not know what game you're playing, how to win and what the score is until it's far too late.

Annual appraisals can cause more harm than good

It wasn't until Christmas a few years ago, when I had breakfast with a senior executive from one of the UK's top companies, that I realised how entrenched this shit is. We'll call him Graham. I laughed when he told me about his annual appraisal. Here's how our conversation went.

> **Graham:** Why are you laughing?

> **Me:** I just assumed that people had wised up to the fact that these appraisals are such a waste of time that they've stopped doing them.

> **Graham:** They still do them in my company, and I was told that I'm a B-player.

> **Me:** That's very nice of your boss to tell you that. Why aren't you an A-player?

> **Graham:** Well, over the last twelve months, I haven't done any of the things he was expecting me to do.

> **Me:** Well, that's brilliant, isn't it? So nice of him to let you know at the end of the year when you can't change anything, instead of talking with you along the way.

Graham: But not only that, it's much worse. When I looked at my objectives for the year, I thought I had done them all. So my boss not only didn't give me any feedback throughout the year, until the end, but our understandings of my objectives were totally different. It was really insulting, because he obviously thinks that I'm so stupid that I've spent the entire year doing the wrong things on purpose.

Graham didn't get a pay raise or a promotion, though he felt he deserved one. Plus, he went away from that meeting totally demoralised and demotivated. And guess what his boss did to rub salt in the wound? He wrote out new objectives that were so vague that Graham knows the same thing will happen again next year.

This excellent employee, who was poached from another company and was extremely competent, felt that the process had done him over and that there was no way to change it. He left that meeting upset and cynical about his job. It was a total waste of time. Graham said that the company would've been better off not having the appraisal because the week before he loved his job, and now he hates it.

What's worse is that he lost respect for his boss. He said to me, 'My boss didn't give me any feedback for twelve months, *and* he thinks I haven't done any of the things he told me to do, which I did. But his objectives were so poorly written, he didn't recognise all that I had accomplished. How can I respect someone who doesn't give me the information I need throughout the year and can't write clear objectives?'

Graham wanted to refute what was said, but he knew that probably would have ruined his relationship with his boss. In most cases like this, there's no place to go to make an appeal. This is a common scenario, and it is frequently the case that companies have all these demoralised employees walking around, while upper management wonders why productivity is in the shitter.

I had this experience myself many years ago in my job at a British retail chain. My manager sat me down for my six-month appraisal. She said that I was doing a horrible job and that I would likely be fired if things didn't change. I was devastated. Completely caught off guard, I had no idea where this had come from because I hadn't had any feedback since I started the job. How could I have known I was doing something wrong? It was outrageous. In the meeting, I just sat and cried. I knew that if I had been told about something that needed to change, I would've fixed it. Thankfully, the company had an appeals process – many companies don't. I made an appeal to the regional office, and they agreed to reassess me at another store.

I appealed because I had nothing to lose. Most people can't take that risk. They just have to live with a flawed appraisal that can sully their career. Not to mention that a company can lose remarkable talent. By the way, after two weeks at the other store, I received glowing feedback, which resulted in me being sent to one of the company's top-performing stores.

The Deloitte and Cisco studies

I've been looking for quite some time, and I can't find any scientific research that shows that an annual appraisal scheme raises performance. Anywhere! So, why are they done? I have a theory.

Small and medium-sized enterprises think they should emulate what larger corporations do. They hear that larger companies do annual appraisals and immediately copy them. They usually copy a bad thing badly. A larger company may do annual appraisals on top of a system of weekly check-ins and quarterly appraisals. But a smaller company blindly replicates one part of the system and not the rest. They often implement an appraisal process because they know that as the company gets bigger, employee performance management is crucial for proving that someone was justly fired. Yet this can be accomplished through other means. It's easier to gauge staff performance issues through weekly check-ins than through an annual appraisal – and frankly, if someone needs to be let go in June, you don't want or need to wait until December.

Various studies show that these annual appraisals are completely ineffective and are a waste of valuable time and effort. Marcus Buckingham and Ashley Goodall, two expert analysts, were hired by *Harvard Business Review* (*HBR*) to study the best way to do annual appraisals. They came back with dismal results: annual appraisals are basically worthless.[47] Their research shook up the business world, so *HBR* asked them to write a book about the entire world of work, not just appraisals. *Nine Lies About Work* was the result, addressing common myths about work, productivity, corporate culture and leadership.[48] In one of their studies, Buckingham and Goodall explained how their work with Deloitte led to an entire change in the appraisal system. Having realised that their established process, annual 360 feedback, was wasting 2 million hours per year, and that employees' performance levels were also dropping drastically, they wanted to implement something that tackled present performance rather than past activity.[49]

In their research, Buckingham and Goodall also looked at Cisco to try to find the ideal cadence for manager and employee one-to-one check-ins. They discovered that weekly check-ins had the best impact on employee engagement and productivity. Fortnightly check-ins weren't as good, and monthly ones were less impactful. Six-weekly was even worse. And if you checked in less frequently than every six weeks, it had a negative impact, because it conveyed to the employee that you didn't care about them or their work. But it was the annual appraisal that had the worst score in terms of enhancing employee engagement and productivity. This is why Buckingham and Goodall open their book with a quote attributed to Mark Twain: 'It ain't what you know that gets you into trouble. It's what you know for sure, that just ain't so.' Those who believe that annual appraisals are helpful are putting their faith in a myth.

The best cadence for reviews

Leaders often ask what I believe is the best cadence for reviews. I suggest their system includes the following four touchpoints:

- A daily huddle or stand-up
- A weekly one-to-one or check-in
- A monthly meeting
- A quarterly meeting for setting objectives

Quarterly objectives should be set for an employee, not annual objectives. They should know what they need to do in the next ninety days. And those objectives should be broken down into at least monthly chunks, if not into thirteen weekly chunks (13 x 7 =

91 days). The employee then reviews progress against those objectives in their weekly meeting with their manager.

This real-time coaching is invaluable and gives the employee tangible steps to take that day or week. These weekly check-ins also prevent annual spikes in activity because they're part of your weekly schedule. No lines of people to meet with and pages of paperwork to file at the end of the year. Instead, the weekly check-ins are a part of the normal routine, and there's no dreaded end-of-the-year reporting taking place.

People want a coach, not a manager

Weekly check-ins should be about coaching, not managing. One of my philosophies that has driven success in check-ins I have led is that you turn managers into coaches. This is great, because nobody wants to be managed. People want autonomy, but they need to know what you want them to achieve so that they can gain a sense of satisfaction.

Can you think of a great piece of work that you did because you were tightly managed? If you ask someone, 'Would you like to be managed?', nine times out of ten, they will say, 'No, but it might be nice if somebody helped me get better at this or that.' Once they know what's expected of them and that they can go to their supervisor for help, people flourish. In sports, a coach helps the athlete to improve his performance. They don't manage them in a command-and-control manner, which we know is ineffective. The coach listens to the athlete, watches their performance and offers guidance.

The appraisal system is fundamentally flawed because it's the manager telling the employee what the manager thinks about the employee. It's not the employee telling the manager what they thought of themselves and asking the manager to be a coach to help them get better. We're acting as though the manager, who sees a tiny fraction of the employee's work, knows the employee better than he knows himself.

OKRs are better than annual appraisals

When companies move to a system of objectives and key results (OKRs), the employee clearly knows the following essential three components:

- The important things to do

- How to measure success

- When to achieve their objectives by

Google uses the OKRs system to create alignment and engagement around measurable goals. John Doerr explains this in detail in his book *Measure What Matters*.[50] A goal describes what you'll achieve and how you're going to measure its accomplishment, and it's evaluated quarterly.

Felipe Castro, who also writes about Google's approach to goal setting, explains that 'by using shorter goal cycles, companies can adapt and respond to change.'[51] In addition, while the company sets the purpose, 'big, hairy, audacious goals' (BHAG™), strategy and values, the team or team member sets the tactical goals.[52] This way, the information is flowing in both directions – top down and bottom up. Rather than cascading down, input from players on the ground ensures that the goals are realistic, attainable and concrete. Most of the time, employees know better than the manager what needs to be done, since they're the 'boots on the ground'. They have a part in setting their own goals (unlike the parent–child approach of annual appraisals).

This system also advocates decoupling compensation and promotions from attaining these goals. Why? Because employees won't set ambitious goals if they fear losing money. As Castro writes, 'OKR is a management tool, not an employee evaluation tool.'[53] It's important to note that OKRs are not task lists. They're priorities. Once the employee knows what is expected of them and has had a hand in setting their goals, they're far more likely to succeed with these tangible steps rather than waiting for some irrelevant evaluation at the end of the year.

Employee engagement and productivity skyrockets when this is implemented correctly, companywide. When every employee has several daily key performance indicators (KPIs), at the end of the week they can meet with their manager and report on their work. They can say, 'I've had a B-week. Can you help me have a better week next week? This is where I need your help.'

Check-ins are the employee's meeting, not the manager's meeting, unlike the annual appraisal, where you're called in to see your manager and your manager gives an evaluation of you, often based on extremely limited data and perspectives. It's done and dusted. The employee can't provide valuable feedback nor contradict the diktats coming down from on high.

So, between the top-down approach (no input from the employee), the cadence (once a year), and the lack of clarity (no clear or agreed-upon objectives for weekly or quarterly work), the annual appraisal system is f**ked up! Remember my friend Graham? The top-down approach, the cadence, and the lack of clarity all contributed to his lack of motivation after his annual appraisal. F**k annual appraisals and embrace weekly check-ins!

Real-time scores are necessary

At one point, when I was MD at Rackspace Technology, the sales team performance wasn't where I wanted it to be. I looked at the data and found that the best salesperson spent four hours a day on the phone. I calculated that a minute of phone time with a prospective client was worth a pound of monthly recurring revenue (MRR). But the rest of the sales team was averaging less than two hours a day on the phone. I then asked the team, 'What do you think is the minimum amount of phone time a Rackspace salesperson should complete each day in order to keep their job?' After a team huddle, they agreed that three hours should be the minimum amount of time, and I showed them what the impact of that would be – doubling sales!

Now, we were all clear on what we measured each day. We displayed the scores in real time on a big monitor on the wall so that every salesperson could see how many minutes they had spent on the phone the previous day. The results? Productivity went up. Sales went up. And those who couldn't make the cut left the company. They knew they weren't able to do what was required of them.

The rest hit their goals and engagement, and efficiency spiked dramatically. It's as Bill Gates once said, 'We all need people who will give us feedback. That's how we improve.'[54] In this case, it was a team seeing some simple metrics on the TV, but it was feedback, nonetheless.

Radical candour is absolutely essential

In her book *Radical Candor: How to get what you want by saying what you mean*, Kim Scott argues that managers must be candid with their employees and vice versa.[55] She explains that radical candour is not brutal honesty or obnoxious aggression. Instead, it's being honest about a person's performance in a way that is empathetic, because work *is* personal. It is a big part of who we are, and we often take criticism personally. But people who care about their jobs want to do a good job, so they need honest feedback to help them grow and improve. The following quote by Frank Clark astutely captures this idea: 'Criticism, like rain, should be gentle enough to nourish a man's growth without destroying his roots.'

Radical candour is essential. We must move away from gossip and innuendo. We must stop talking negatively about another teammate if they're not present. Speaking behind a person's back won't help that person, and it will harm your reputation. You'll be seen as a gossip and a coward. Colleagues need to be able to give one another honest feedback.

Another important thing to remember is that the higher a leader goes up in the organisation, the more approachable they must be. Without candid conversations, the leader will remain in a bubble, oblivious to what's going on and what decisions are needed. You don't need to surround yourself with yes-men. You need honest feedback about yourself and the issues the company faces.

When coaching, I often ask people the following three questions:

1. Would you tell a colleague if they had spinach in their teeth?

    - 70% say yes.

    - 30% say no.

2. Would you tell a colleague if their fly was down or if their skirt was caught in their knickers?

    - 50% say yes.

    - 50% say no.

3. Would you tell a colleague if they smelled bad or had bad breath?

    - 30% say yes.

    - 70% say no.

Did you notice that the responses changed? My theory is that the questions get more personal, and people are more reluctant to tell someone else the uncomfortable truth.

I then ask three follow-up questions:

1. What if your colleague realises he's had spinach in his teeth all day, and you've sat next to him all day without saying a word?

2. What if your colleague arrives at the pub and their friend tells them their fly is down, or their skirt is tucked into their knickers, and they realise it has been like that for hours?

3. What if your colleague goes home and their spouse tells them that they stink?

The people I speak with usually get it. With the second round of questions, they realise that the colleague will likely be disappointed that no one said anything until it was too late.

In the same way, even though work is personal, people need valuable, candid feedback to help them change, develop and improve. For most managers, giving feedback is similar to the response about body odour and not the spinach. They're too embarrassed to have difficult conversations. They must have the courage and candour needed to speak up and help people grow. Their business depends on it.

Be open to giving and receiving honest feedback

People think they're straightforward, but most people aren't. They have a tough time being direct with others about their faults, poor performance, incorrect behaviour or faux pas. They'll tell you that they want to be straightforward and that they admire people who are. But when push comes to shove, they aren't straightforward. They fear having hard conversations.

A manager's job is to help their employee become the best version of themselves that they can be. That can't happen if a leader avoids the tough conversations that are needed to help an employee recognise what kinds of behaviour undermine their strengths. Only once they know what to work on can they continue to improve.

Another example comes to mind from my early time at Rackspace. We created a reward for employees where we'd pay for a weekend away at a hotel as a reward for the best employee of the quarter. During that time, I noticed that an employee was really struggling. Let's call him Daniel. He was at the bottom of the pack. The feedback I received was that Daniel never answered the phone. When the phone rang, he looked the other way and faked looking busy. I told him this. I said, 'Daniel, you're at the bottom of the ranking because you never answer the phone.' Straightforward feedback. Transparent feedback. Candour. Guess what happened in the next quarter? He was employee of the quarter, and people complained that they never got to speak to a customer because Daniel always answered the phone.

This simple, real-time feedback transformed Daniel, and it will do the same for the people you coach. I've noticed that it's easier for people to give and receive feedback when a culture is created for this to happen. It's just a normal part of your weekly check-ins. And, when the context has to do with daily (real-time) struggles based on scores and not some one-time event at the end of the year, it's easier for people to seek out or receive critical feedback. This is why Ed Batista writes, 'Make feedback normal. Not a performance review.' [56]

No triangulation

At Peer 1 Hosting, we came up with an agreement at the executive team level that transformed the organisation. We called it 'No triangulation'. We agreed that if one person complained to another about someone or had concerns about that person, then the complainer had seventy-two hours to have a conversation directly with the individual about that concern. If they didn't, the third person would. Now, sometimes people need space like that to blow off some steam or to get some advice about a difficult employee. The rule can be summed up as, 'Never have a negative conversation about anyone without them in the room.' After we adopted this behaviour, we in time rolled it down throughout the organisation. In essence, people knew that negative conversations behind someone's back wouldn't be tolerated. It changed the workplace into a healthier and safe environment, with one less thing to worry about. We built a culture that frowned on complaining and gossiping. And if people transgressed this code, we had a reason to let them go, since they knew they'd violated company culture.

One time, a global leader (we'll call him Bob) shared with me some problems he was having with a sales director (we'll call her Olivia). I told Bob that he had seventy-two hours to talk to Olivia. He didn't, and I kept my end of the bargain and had a conversation with Olivia about the concerns. Bob said, 'I can't believe you told her what I told you!' I replied, 'I told you that's how we behave in this company.' Bob soon left the organisation. He simply couldn't have the challenging conversations that were needed. He couldn't commit to 'No triangulation'. And while he had many strengths, if this was the kind of culture we wanted to create for engagement and productivity, it was best for him to work elsewhere. He couldn't commit to radical candour, and as I said before, it's essential.

If you can't create a culture where people are having difficult conversations, then you're going to be mediocre. No professional sports team has a shrinking violet as a coach. The coach must be able to say, 'Sam, you played horribly today. You know you can do better. How can I help you?'

I've seen it time and time again. You can take this to the bank: businesses will only survive if people can have difficult conversations.

Key questions about your annual appraisal system

I expect that some readers of this chapter might still keep their annual appraisal systems. If that's you, or if you're not yet convinced that you need to completely revamp your appraisal process, here are some key questions to ask yourself:

- How does my annual appraisal system help me to reward excellent performance?

- Do my employees really know what's expected of them through this system?

- Without my current annual employee appraisal system, would I know who my best performers are?

- Does my annual appraisal system actually motivate my employees?

- Since I implemented my annual appraisal system, has employee productivity increased?

- Did I only implement the annual appraisal system so that I can justify firing low-performing people?

Summary

- Annual appraisals are a complete waste of everyone's time. Real-time feedback is of far greater value as employees can make changes immediately. Ditch your yearly performance review and implement weekly check-ins. Do it today!

- People want a coach, not a manager. Give your employees a chance to input into their own objectives and performance evaluation by using OKRs. Remember the 'idiosyncratic rater' effect – why do we have so much trust in the rater's evaluation when it is never objective?

- Short-term goals are more effective than annual targets.

- Get comfortable with honesty. Implement a culture of radical candour and embrace honest feedback.

- Healthy communication between employees is essential. Introduce a 'no triangulation' policy. If your employees can't hack it, show them the door.

- If you're still not ready to get rid of your annual appraisals process, ask yourself why. How is it serving you? Do you need to face some uncomfortable truths?

6

As You Scale, Don't Specialise Into Functions

You're populating your business with A-players, but how should you organise them? Consider following the advice of Robin Dunbar, a British anthropologist who studied the size and capacity of the human brain as well as research from various fields such as psychology and archaeology. He concluded that no company unit should be larger than 150 people (148 to be precise). He looked back in history and noticed that the largest population of a village during the Neolithic period was about 150. This was the same size as the basic unit of the Roman army and Hutterite settlements. Modern armies organise in a similar way.

Dunbar's number theory is that humans can't have a three-dimensional relationship with more than 150 people, and we feel a sense of community when groups are smaller in number than that. Dunbar states, 'The figure of 150 seems to represent the maximum number of individuals with whom we can have a genuinely social relationship, the kind of relationship that goes with knowing who they are and how they relate to us.'

A small team of seven people may be ideal. But even when you put all of your teams together, no unit should go above Dunbar's number. WL Gore, the makers of Gore-Tex, don't have more than 150 employees in the same building for this reason. It's easier to foster a sense of community and mission when the combined units are no larger than 150 people – if the group is larger than this, we may feel disconnected and lost in the crowd.[57] In addition, we're less likely to keep our promises because we're dealing with nameless, faceless people. Integrity and excellence diminish because our work has been depersonalised.

Dunbar also claims that you spend 40% of your time with five people and you spend 20% of your time with ten people. So you spend about 60% of your time with just fifteen people. For this reason, it's best to be a part of a small team and to have a customer-facing cohort that focuses on a smaller group of clients.

There's also the Ringelmann Effect. This is the tendency of individuals in a group to become less productive as the size of the group increases. French agricultural engineer Maximilien Ringelmann created an experiment and asked volunteers to pull on a rope. He found that when only one person is pulling on the rope, they give all their effort. However, when more people are added, individual effort decreases.[58]

Social loafing

Alan Ingham came up with the concept of 'social loafing' from recreating this experiment. He found that individual effort decreases as team size increases.[59] Why? Because of each team member's thought process that they don't need to work as hard – there are other people there to pick up the slack, and besides, how will they know how much effort each person is putting in?

As Jacob Morgan writes in his *Forbes* article, 'Why smaller teams are better than larger ones': 'The same concept explains why many people don't vote, why bystanders don't take action when needed, or why some people within teams slack off.'[60] In a large group, people feel that their individual effort won't matter to the group. Morgan also writes about the Gallup study that showed that workers were more engaged at smaller companies than larger companies.

So, the larger your team, the less effort you may see from your employees. Large teams are notorious for having 'social loafers', but it's difficult to be a slacker in a small team. Well, there's one exception. If the manager is a slacker, then a team member can slack off. Besides that, smaller teams bring greater accountability and output.

The Ringelmann Effect and social loafing can get people killed. Twenty-six US soldiers died on April 14, 1994, when two US Air Force F-15 fighters accidentally shot down two US Army Black Hawk helicopters over northern Iraq. West Point Professor Scott Snook analysed the incident in his book *Friendly Fire*. Snook stated that social loafing was a contributing factor to the failure of the aircraft team to track the helicopters and prevent them being shot down. Snook asserted that responsibility was 'spread so thin by the laws of social impact and confused authority relationships that no one felt compelled to act.'[61]

Forgive me for being a bit dramatic, but you get the point. If people are less engaged as the team size increases because they think their contribution isn't important, it can have catastrophic effects.

Don't build an empire, build small teams

If you want to build an empire, don't try to run a business. Sure, there are the Jeff Bezos and Sundar Pichais of the world. But, to run a successful business, you can't always think big. The desire to control everything, along with the illusion that the biggest companies are always better, will make it hard for people to accept this truth: as you grow bigger, you need to think smaller. Don't build large departments. Build small teams.

There are countless advantages to small teams, as I'll share throughout this chapter. According to a Xero article entitled 'The secret power of small teams', 'In a group of 5–8 people everyone has a chance to speak, raise unusual ideas, and collaborate... One of the best things about working in small teams is that brilliant ideas can go into action immediately.'[62] Certainly, the fewer people involved in decision-making the quicker decisions can be implemented.

Typically, everyone starts off as multifunctional in smaller companies. But as organisations grow, employees specialise into departments, destroying communication, efficiency and customer satisfaction. Teams are inefficient and ineffective, not to mention isolated.

The solution is to build small, multidisciplinary teams that are efficient and effective. Don't build your organisation along functions or departments. Build your organisation with small teams composed of diverse functions that deliver value to a defined group of customers.

Let's look at an example. A debt collector (let's call him Ron) may work in a 'silo' where debt collection is his team's focus. Job function: collect debt. Period. That's all he's been exposed to and supposed to do. He's disassociated from the impact of poorly implemented credit collection and how it destroys customer satisfaction, resulting in hundreds of one-star reviews. But if Ron were moved into a small team in which he did multiple tasks, he would soon develop a well-rounded view of the company and its goals. This would in turn cause Ron to realise that collecting money, which is now his only focus, is not as important as the overall goal, which is to care for customers and to ensure that the company's reputation is upheld.

Small teams like this don't need special information-sharing tools. They don't have to write as much down because they know what everyone is doing and can soon finish one another's sentences. Small-team members get into a rhythm with one another, so fewer meetings, memos and metrics are needed.

But these kinds of teams are seldom formed because the standard practice is to specialise into functions as you scale. When a company grows from ten people to 100, generalists turn into specialists. The person who used to wear seven hats now needs to wear only one. And she has plenty of work to do in the more specialised area. So people are placed into silos, teams grow larger, and small cohorts of diverse team members slowly fade away. What was a natural cohort in a smaller company becomes accidentally extinct as departments narrow their contribution to specific functions.

Dashun Wang and James A Evans from *Harvard Business Review* devoted years to studying the pros and cons of large and small teams. They discovered that large teams were more prone to communication difficulties and resistant to innovation. They were more risk averse, wanting to tread familiar ground to maintain their standard outputs in established channels of their operation. Meanwhile, small teams, like startups, were more likely to try out new things, as doing so was less risky and offered so much potential.

Wang and Evans examined over 65 million papers, patents and software projects to explore the effects of team size. They concluded that, while large teams excelled at problem-solving, 'it is small teams that are more likely to come up with new problems for their more sizable counterparts to solve. Work by large teams tends to build on more recent, popular ideas, while small teams reach further into the past, finding inspiration in more obscure prior ideas and possibilities.'[63] They agree with Jeff Bezos, who operated the two-pizza team rule: if you can't feed a team with two pizzas, it's too large.[64]

Tear down the walls

Companies assume that the best way to organise specialists is by putting them in their own departments. So, there's the sales department, the marketing department, the operations department, the social media department, and so forth. The salespeople think that all the leads from marketing are horrible. Marketing think everybody in sales is lazy and that they never follow up on any of the leads they send through. Everybody in sales thinks operations is the 'no' department. Operations believe that the sales department is overpromising and underdelivering. Tribalism flourishes as people from different departments rarely work together.

But what if people from these disparate departments could work together on a small team? The cross-pollination of knowledge and skills could have a dramatic effect on the company. Disunity and rigid specialisation could turn into unity and integration. Walls would be broken down between departments, and they could function with increased awareness, precision and purpose.

Don't get me wrong, there will always be functions in the organisation that can't be blended into small teams because there are too few experts. Perhaps the team responsible for M&A stays as its own team. The customer-facing functions can be blended to create various pods, stripes or squads (small teams) aligned to varying customer cohorts. In software development the function can have multidisciplinary teams building elements of the software and being internally responsible for product, scrum, development, UX and QA – just as they do at Spotify.[65]

Having a BHAG™ (Big Hairy Audacious Goal, or the company's mission), purpose and core values are so important. If leaders or managers align their employees around core values, then they shouldn't behave in a disconnected way, even if they're not part of a smaller team.

Embodying values creates happy and healthy teams

Allow me to share an example of how embodying values can contribute to a better workforce, regardless of the size of the team. It was drawn to my attention by the young female workforce at Rackspace that the company's purpose was fanatical support. They were right – we had even trademarked the term, Fanatical Support®! They also pointed out that our BHAG was to be renowned as one of the greatest service companies in the world. Again, they were correct. Then they stuck in the dagger: 'So why is our maternity pay so terrible? It's just the statutory minimum. That doesn't seem fanatical to us.'

I told them they were right, and that this policy was discordant with our purpose. We are passionate about hiring and retaining A-player talent, and we should offer better care and support for our employees. None of the women were pregnant, but they said they were looking down the road and knew that they might have children within the next few years. They were hesitant to recommit to the company with this concern hanging over their heads.

So much evidence shows that businesses lose billions of pounds' worth of talented employees because they don't come back to work after maternity leave. Some of the women I worked with suggested that, after having the baby, they would feel more confident about returning to work if they could return on a part-time basis. I told them, 'Done.' But I also told them to investigate what 'best in class' looks like for maternity leave and to create a proposal. I promised them that whatever they proposed, I would accept.

So often, people get to prepare a proposal for their boss so that their boss, who hasn't done any research on the subject, can make it 'better'. I tell people, 'Your proposal is pre-approved. You did the investigation, so I won't try to make it better.' People feel the weight of this responsibility. They own it. My female employees went away, came up with an outstanding proposal, and stayed on as happy employees because of how we cared for and supported them. That was several years ago, and many of them are still at Rackspace.

Smaller teams create greater customer satisfaction

At Rackspace, we called them teams. At Peer 1 Hosting, we called them pods. At itlab, we called them stripes. At other companies, they call them squads.

Whatever you call them, these small teams can be incredibly effective at creating top-tier customer service. In a traditional department-aligned company, it would be difficult to do what we did. But at itlab, we picked our top ten customers and realised that they were responsible for about 30% of the company's revenue. The next fifty customers brought in another 30%, and the last 150 generated about the same. We had 650 non-contractual customers who brought in about 10% of our revenue.

We assigned one person to manage those 650 customers. Many companies don't quantify this data, so they are spending disproportionate time and work on customers who bring in little revenue. Before we changed our configuration of teams, we would have some of our biggest customers in a queue, waiting to speak to an engineer, behind a few customers who hardly paid any money and didn't have a contract. So we created a team that was dedicated to our top ten customers. We had our top engineers, technical talent, client advocate, business development consultant and IT manager ready to help them.

We ended up assigning one-third of the company's customer-facing employees to those top ten customers. They still did their functional work, but we sat them together. We had them huddle every morning and work together to support those crucial clients.

Rather than the team members thinking functionally ('I'm just an engineer'), we had them thinking about the customer and working as a cohesive group, bringing their strengths together to offer the best customer service possible. Again, they still had their engineering, marketing, IT, and other specialised work to do. But because they sat together and worked together as a team, they were able to bring those skills together for the customers in a way that couldn't have happened if they had been operating in single-function departments that doubled as silos.

We made the job more personal for everyone on that team. The business consultant knew that she was only selling to ten customers. She didn't have a mix of big and small clients in terms of complexity. And when she solved a problem for one of those more influential customers, she could pass on that knowledge to others who focused on smaller clients. She saw the impact of her skills on the customers and her team members in a unique way.

We also assigned key workers from credit control to this top-ten team. This way, when a ticket was raised, it didn't go to some random person in the finance team. It went to someone who knew they were part of the team that served our top ten customers. This small-team configuration radically transformed customer satisfaction, and in just twenty-four months, their NPS went from −7 to +55.

Small-team advantages

I've also seen how small teams band together in unique ways. A smaller team has a common purpose and level of intimacy that often leads them to come in early or stay late to get the job done. There's a deeper level of accountability, which means the manager or coach has less managing or coaching to do. When that small team helps with hiring, the results are always better. They don't want to hire anyone who will disturb the camaraderie and trust of the group. A small team will give you vital input because they want to protect their 'family'. And if I ask this team to write their processes, they will always be better than diktats from corporate because the procedures will be specific to a particular group and not some generic idea that may not apply to other departments or teams. They're not trying to boil the ocean, so the result will be better than some document handed down from on high.

When companies listen to my advice, they'll often decentralise departments. They'll have central marketing focus on branding, but they move lead generation to smaller teams in regions and take it out of the hands of central marketing.

More importantly, small teams are better for the customer. When customers ring up, most of the time they'll speak with the same person. The customers then have a more personal relationship with the company, and the employees know what our customers need and how best to interact with them because they have built a rapport with them.

Even though the company may be large, when customers call in, they feel like they've just gone down to the village shop and the owner is there ready with their usual order. The employee can say, 'How are you doing, Bob? Last time we spoke, your daughter was going into surgery. How is she doing? I also wanted to ask you how things were going with your new printer since we installed it two weeks ago.' The employee knows the customer so well that they know what to say and what not to say. There's also another benefit: as you measure how various teams are succeeding, you can dive in and pull out best practices that may help struggling teams.

The power of culture

Never underestimate the power of culture. It tells people what we value, what's expected, and what behaviours won't be tolerated. When we create culture in a company, people are formed in their thinking and actions. And the culture that is created can be more effective than the best leader in the world.

For instance, Professor Moira Clark, from Henley Business School, carried out a project with a high-street bank in Sheffield. She took the manager from the best branch and put them in the worst branch. This manager was unable to make any substantial changes.

Professor Clark found that a tipping point was only reached when 30% of people from the best branch were transplanted into the worst branch to make any positive changes.[66]

My view is that the power of bad is about four times more powerful than the power of good. One bad apple can spoil the bunch. One good apple doesn't fix the bad ones. That said, when the bad apples in the business see a strong leader plus experience a culture that's developed by good workers, they eventually either get on board or leave.

How to identify the health of your teams

As the CEO of your company or a leader of a team, how do you *really* know what is and isn't working? I recommend simply surveying each of your departments (eg marketing, sales, finance, R&D, customer support). Consider asking certain employees the following questions:

- How good do you think your department is at delivering to your customers (or to other departments in the company)?

- How good do you think you are at delivering service to your team?

- How good are your colleagues at delivering service to you?

- How good do you think other departments in your company are at delivering to their customers (or to you and other departments)?

If there's a perception gap in your business, the above questions will uncover it. The perception gap can sometimes be summarised as an 'it's not me, it's them' mentality. In other words, people incorrectly think that they're doing a great job and everyone else is doing a poor job.

Then ask the same employees the following questions:

- In the past, when you worked on an efficient and effective team, what did it look like?
- Tell me about the best team you were on. It could be a sports team, a team at work, a team that did charitable work or activism, or some other team.
- What were some of its characteristics?

Answers to the previous questions will reveal how inefficient and ineffective large departments are (with no teams) and will remind people what efficient and effective small teams are like.

Typically, answers will include gems such as the following:

- 'We were connected.'
- 'There was a clear sense of mission and purpose.'

- 'We worked so well together.'

- 'There were consequences for non-compliance.'

- 'Nobody was slacking off, there was a high level of commitment, and people kept their promises.'

- 'We were aligned around a core purpose.'

From well-managed to self-managed

In many cases, well-managed teams become self-managing, and end up needing very little oversight. This is how Spotify organises things, for example. Their small teams self-manage.

The Spotify organisational model was first introduced in 2012 when Henrik Kniberg and Anders Ivarsson published the white paper 'Scaling Agile @ Spotify'.[67] This introduced the world to the radically simple way Spotify approached organisational agility at scale. Unsurprisingly, Spotify doesn't leverage the original implementation of the Spotify Agile model anymore; they evolved and adapted an updated model to fit their changing organisation.

In essence, we're taking lessons we've learned from software development and the agile revolution and bringing it to general business. In my years as a consultant, I have seen incredible results when companies stop building large departments and start building small teams.

Summary

- Research has shown time and again that smaller groups are more efficient than larger groups. Dunbar's number puts the ideal number of a team at fewer than 150 people.

- The Ringelmann effect shows that when more people are put to a task, their individual effort decreases. Social loafing is a problem for productivity and can have catastrophic consequences.

- Small, multidisciplinary teams are more efficient than larger, single-function departments. Don't be afraid to shake things up – you could revolutionise your organisation.

- Happy teams make happy customers. Your teams should embody your company culture. Let them tell you what benefits they want, and pre-approve them to show them you trust their judgement.

- Assign your best people to your best customers. If only a handful of customers are making you a large proportion of revenue, dedicate a small team to them and them only. Watch your profitability grow.

- Gather feedback from your teams about what's working and do more of it. The best teams manage themselves with low input needed from management – transform them from well-managed to self-managed groups.

7
How To Identify And Test-Run Future Leaders

One morning in Bournemouth, I was sipping a hot cup of coffee at a conference. I was still waking up, not entirely engaged, when a speaker said something that made me sit up and take notice. Nadya Powell said, 'We have loads of people who are shit leaders and loads of people who think their leaders are shit. But soon they will become a leader, and because they don't have any decent role models, they will be shit.'[68]

I kept asking myself, 'Why is this so true?' I've seen terrible leaders. I've seen people who hated their bosses, and then I've seen those same people become hated bosses. Likewise, I was struck by the fact that there's a circle of life, but it's more like a circle of death in the corporate world. Then I realised that leaders don't magically appear. They're usually promoted. And people are often promoted to the level of their incompetence.

It's called 'The Peter Principle' and was 'discovered' way back in 1969 by Dr Laurence J Peter. We don't seem to have learned from his principle, even after all these decades, because it is still the case that after being promoted to a new position, a staggering number of people end up failing, as described in Dr Peter's book, *The Peter Principle*.[69]

People are promoted based on success in their previous role, but they'll eventually reach a level that leads to failure. Why? Because they either have never had the coaching needed to succeed in this new role, or because the skills in one role do not translate to the new role. Here are two examples to think about:

1. **Sales:** A great salesperson might be promoted to the role of a district sales manager, but sales and management are quite different. Just because someone excels in sales doesn't mean they'll likewise thrive as a manager. The first role requires selling skills, the second requires the love and the skills to coach others.

2. **Technology:** It's laudable to want to promote from within, but your best software developer may be the last person who should ever become your chief technology officer. The new position

requires additional talent, skills, emotional intelligence and good instincts.

Failure at some level is so inevitable that Dr Peter encouraged his readers to feign incompetence to retain their current position. Too many leaders are promoted too soon, which leads to failure. Not much has changed since the 1960s, which is why this chapter will help you avoid common potholes along the road to promotion.

Promote people who are already doing the work

If you want to promote people successfully, elevate people who are already doing the work they'll need to do in their new position. Obviously, this can't always be observed, as their new role will require a different focus or responsibilities than their current one. But there are some ways that you'll be able to see certain traits that cross over from one position to another. You'll also be able to observe the specific skills and attitudes that will be needed in this person's new role.

While at Rackspace, we hired a load of graduates straight out of university. One in particular, Lucy, struggled to understand the job and to get her work done. Another team member, Clarissa, came in early to coach Lucy and stayed late to finish her own work. I noticed Clarissa doing this for quite some time and was impressed by her initiative, selflessness, concern for the company's success, and her diligence. When a sales manager position opened up, Clarissa got it because she was naturally doing the work that was required in her new position.

One of the other team members asked me, 'Why can't I apply for the position?'

I said, 'You can, but you're not going to get it because you're a salesperson, and you've regularly hit your sales numbers. That's fine, but I'm looking for someone who goes beyond that.'

'Well,' she said, 'if you made me a manager, then I'd do coaching.'

No. You don't do the work because you get the job title. You get the job and the title because you do the work. I politely explained this to her, and she couldn't deny that Clarissa was better suited for the position based on her proven performance.

You have to find examples of people doing the work you need them to do. That should be the standard for promotion – not seniority, time served, or being good at a particular function. Granted, salespeople need to focus on sales, and they're not paid to do the work of a manager. But if you look closely enough, you'll see that the cream rises to the top. You'll catch people demonstrating abilities that are needed for one position while they're working in another. Keep in mind too that your best managers may not even be your best salespeople.

Create a test-run for potential leaders

A sure-fire way to determine whether a person can handle a management position is by giving them a test-run. I've created non-management posts where people get to manage cross-functional teams. I've asked people to volunteer as the manager of the charity or culture committee. This way, they get to try out their management skills without impacting revenue. When we announce these volunteer positions, inevitably, those who want to manage step forward and those who are happy to be led stand back.

The person who is selected is observed in this new capacity, and we determine whether they have the raw talent needed to be promoted. We can also see if they need some training or if they simply won't be able to do the job. We don't tell the people that this is a test, but we get to see who functions well in this new role and who doesn't.

There are other ways to discover who may make a great coach or manager. A leader in a company can ask various team members the following question when there's a managerial position opening up: 'We need to identify a manager for this team. Other than yourself, who do you think would be the best for the position?' Once that person is identified, give them opportunities to manage or coach. Observe them as they interact with people and accomplish goals to see if they're really management material.

There is a DDO (deliberately developmental organisation) called Next Jump, which has been featured in the *Harvard Business Review* and a TED Talk for its innovative strategies.[70] Next Jump gives intentional feedback on a worker's backhand. In tennis, a player's backhand swing is almost always weaker than their forehand swing. In business, your backhand is a skill that you need to do your job, but which isn't your strong point. Once your backhand is identified, Next Jump helps you create ways to work on that weakness.

For example, Next Jump does cultural tours of their office space every quarter. During this time, they tell people about the history of Next Jump, its mission, vision, values, culture and its commitments to employees. The team that runs the cultural tours are composed of people who have received feedback that they're weak at public speaking. And they've been told that without improving this skill, it'll be difficult for them to move up the ladder. By taking on the tour-leadership role, they prepare for the promotions they desire.

Coaches and captains

Next Jump structures the cultural tours team uniquely. A captain is put in charge of running the cultural tours. This captain has a coach who was their former captain. The captain has two people who help them. The goal is for the captain to coach the helpers to be the next captain, while a former captain is coaching the captain. And eventually, the captain becomes a coach. People participate in this tour of duty as a captain for about six months. After they get their helpers up to speed, they then serve as a coach for another six months.

This strategy helps a person work on their own weakness and then coach someone who has the same weakness. By managing facilities and recruitment in this way, people get in front of people in a low-risk scenario (with next to no consequences if they fail). These test-runs then reveal whether they're ready for something with more responsibility. It helps them strengthen their backhand.

There are other ways to get people to step up while giving them a safety net. I could tell an employee, 'I'd like to make you a manager, but it's a temporary position, and for now, there's no pay raise.' Why would I do this? Because so often in companies, Charlie gets a new title, a new salary, their partner starts spending the extra money, but when we see that Charlie can't do the job, there's nowhere for them to go but to leave the company. It's too late or too difficult for Charlie to move back down the ladder, swallow their pride, change their title back and reduce their salary.

Charlie may have been promoted because they're the best software developer or salesperson. But, after this fiasco, you'll lose them rather than retain them in their old position, which would likely have been ideal for them and the company. If you create situations where a person must either succeed or leave, and success is a 50/50 proposition (at best), then you're just building a pipeline for losing some of your best talent.

Typically, an employee appreciates being able to take this temporary Tour of Duty with everyone's eyes wide open, so that a valuable test-run has taken place before any large or permanent changes go into effect.[71] The test-run enables people to walk away and go back to their job if needed. It also helps people save face. We're practising radical candour with Charlie and the company – they know we're giving them a trial run, and then we'll see what happens next. If you think the person has potential, you may offer a bonus after six months. But in general, you're letting them know that a promotion and raise is attainable only if they can first prove that they can do the work.

Test-runs allow you to rewind the clock

At Rackspace, there was an opening for a manager in a tech team. I went to the team and asked, 'If it wasn't you, who do you think should manage this team?' They unanimously named the top performer. We'll call him Harry. I asked Harry if he'd like to take a test-run, and while he had some concerns about the position, he agreed. I told him that if he didn't like the new position or if I felt it wasn't a good fit, we could wind back from it.

He was promoted to manage the system administrator team and was unanimously selected by his colleagues, but he hated weekly one-on-one meetings and other managerial responsibilities. The team also realised that his skill set was better suited for his prior role rather than as a manager. He gladly moved back to his old role, and we were pleased that a top performer stayed.

The test-run enabled us to keep a great employee. It also ensured that we didn't fill his position until the test-run was complete. In many other companies, if he had failed as a manager, he would have had no other choice but to find another job. Somebody else would've already filled his position. But we don't fill those openings until the test-runs are complete, in case the employee needs to go back to their former role. If you don't have a system in place to give you the ability to rewind the clock, you'll either be stuck with the wrong person in a vital role, or you'll lose valuable talent.

Create a peer-coaching programme

Another way to find great managers is by setting up and running a peer-coaching programme. When creating a peer-coaching programme, the leader should ask their employees the following: 'Who would you like to team up with in this peer-coaching programme? In other words, who do you want to be your coach?' By seeing who gets picked the most, you may have some idea of who has the most leadership potential. This becomes incredibly helpful after you've gone through a few rounds of coaching. When a person is picked a few times because 'word of mouth' has spread about how he or she is a fantastic coach, you gain insight into who could be promoted.

On top of that, when you detect that no one has asked Nigel to be their coach, you've just discovered the dark matter in the organisation. If several rounds go by and no one chooses a certain person, that means they're probably not coach or management material. There could be other factors, such as that person may be shy. But in general, who does *not* get picked can tell you just as much as who does.

In a peer-coaching programme, there's the coach and the talent. The talent has to organise the meetings, set the agenda, do the preparatory work, and the coach helps the talent work through a specific problem or challenge. I typically tell the coaches not to come up with solutions for those they're coaching, instead encouraging them to ask many questions and to have the employee come up with solutions as much as possible. If they're keen to learn more on coaching, I suggest that they read Michael Bungay Stanier's book *The Coaching Habit: Say less, ask more and change the way you lead forever.*[72]

The talent must have an objective, such as learning how to improve his or her productivity. It must be a specific, measurable goal that the coach is trying to help them achieve. Through the process, the participants will develop the skills they need to be promoted without having a negative impact on revenue. They will learn how to coach others, develop radical candour, grow in their people skills, hold people accountable and lead a team. A peer-coaching programme is also a dynamic way of moving your company from having a minority of A-player managers to a majority.

This coaching programme doesn't have to be too rigid. Keep it flexible. If there isn't chemistry between two people, make a switch. We usually set it up as a six-month commitment and ask the people to meet once every two weeks for an hour. If the programme needs to be of less than six months' duration or requires more time each meeting, then do that. You can also get the coaches together to share best practices, helping them improve. Have the coaches do some role-playing of various scenarios so that they develop as well as those being coached.

I often coach leaders who say that they now have 300 staff members and are projecting to have 700 staff members in about three years. I'll ask the leaders, 'Do you know who you're going to promote to management to coach or train all these new employees? Do you have a plan for that? Do you have a management training university? Do you have any kind of peer-coaching programme?' Most of the time, they can't answer those questions with an immediate yes.

If you don't want to be a phenomenal company, then don't implement a peer programme. If you want your company to thrive, develop a coaching programme so that all of your managers are having the greatest impact. Remember, managers can impact the majority of their staff's employee engagement scores.

Stop, start, continue

Managers often tell their staff to set some personal development goals, but employees have no idea where to start. With 'stop, start, continue,' they'll know exactly what to do.

If you're being coached, gather your team together, give each person a piece of paper divided into three, and ask them to write down what you should stop doing, start doing and continue doing. You can give this to your coach and ask them to help you work on these traits or behaviours.

This form of feedback helps people become the best version of themselves. When paired with an experienced leader who can help a person grow, the employee's personal development can be quite dramatic.

Unlike traditional forms of review, 'stop, start, continue' focuses on how the employee makes others feel. Anyone can answer a questionnaire about how strategic or motivational someone is, but the results are often misleading because there isn't enough data to back it up. 'Stop, start, continue' enables each person on the team to give their opinion about what another person needs to do to improve. Most of the time, it's far more accurate than a 360-degree review or other more theoretical analyses.

The person being reviewed not only goes over the feedback with their coach, but they then go back to the team a few months later and ask how they're progressing. Over time, as trust builds, people will put their initials on the paper so that additional feedback and clarifications can be pursued.

Coaching vs managing

Henry Stewart, author of *The Happy Manifesto*, often says to his audience, 'I want you to think about the professional work you've done that you're most proud of. Please put your hand up if that work was done as a result of being managed.'[73] Regularly, no hands go up in the room. The perception of management is that of getting people to do things they don't want to do. Managers are seen as taskmasters who drive their people to do what they're paid to do.

Coaches, on the other hand, show the way. They help an employee gain competency. They don't manage them. Coaches focus more on asking the right questions to help people gain more clarity about themselves or their circumstances, rather than giving solutions. They don't just throw out the answer. Coaches help emerging leaders solve the problem themselves. You're teaching people to fish, not giving them a fish.

A theory suggested by MIT's Douglas McGregor in the 1950s assumed that people would hardly do anything at work unless managers compelled them to do specific tasks. These workers needed managers to get the minimum effort out of them so that they didn't get fired. McGregor's theory also said that if you create an environment where people come to labour with other people to do meaningful work, they'll thrive and be joyfully productive.[74]

The latter is an environment where people need coaches, not managers. A coach guides, motivates, engages, or trains. He or she doesn't watch over others or overbearingly compel people to do their work. Showing someone the ropes is different from whipping them with one. Ultimately, we're looking for the best way to work so that we can build a great company that delivers an excellent experience for their customers. Happy staff lead to happy customers, which leads to more profit. Create a test-run for potential leaders, create a peer-coaching programme, and as coaches raise up new and effective leaders, your company will flourish.

Summary

- 'The Peter Principle' dictates that even the best people will be promoted to a level where they don't succeed. To avoid this being a problem in your company, you must be strategic about promotion.

- Promote people who are already doing the work required of the new role. Keep in mind that your best salesperson may not make the best manager, and vice versa. Keep your best salesperson selling and promote the team member who already displays the best management skills.

- Test-runs allow you and your employees to give a promotion a try, without fear of what would happen if it turned out not to be the right move. Employees who can't save face if they struggle after promotion will usually leave – if there's a test-run process in place, you're more likely to keep them if they find out their new role doesn't work for them.

- A peer-coaching programme allows you to improve your workforce from within. You can make managers from existing teams and transform people into A-players. You find out, from peer nomination, who would make a great leader and who wouldn't, and you engage your employees in their own progression process. What's not to like?

- Remember, your team members need coaches, not managers. Foster a culture of mentoring and mutual learning, rather than top-down instruction. Ask leaders to use exercises like 'stop, start, continue' to find out what's working and what needs to change in real time and then have them and their team member do something about it.

8
Offices Need To Reflect Your Company Culture

You have a problem, but you don't know that you have a problem. And those are the worst kinds of problems. How can you solve a problem that you're unaware of? When 'you don't know what you don't know', it's impossible to remedy the situation.

Spoiler alert: the problem is your office space. If your office environment doesn't reflect your company culture and isn't conducive to comfortable and synergistic work, your employees are operating at a significant disadvantage. Without a creative and functional space, you lose opportunities with potential customers and hires.

Your office design could be one of the biggest hindrances to your company's growth. At one company I

worked for, I'd venture to say that we gained a significant percentage of our clients and employees because
of our unique office layout and culture. It not only
won people over when they visited, but it created
an atmosphere for creative, meaningful and effective
work.

No one had their own closed office, even me. The hier-
archy was flat – and it looked this way too. There were
lots of meeting rooms, so there was always space for a
meeting or a quiet conversation. There were also quiet
areas, where deep work could be finished uninter-
rupted. The effect was like having a library where you
could go to work inside the office. We provided great
coffee, so the caffeine was on tap, and we had a 'bring
your dog to work' policy. We even had a pub in the
office for beer o'clock at the end of the day on Friday
afternoons. We located the office within walking dis-
tance of the town centre, so staff could do 'weekend
chores' in their lunch hour. There was enough car
parking space for everyone who drove, indoor cycle
parking for the bikes and public transport links to
buses and trains.

One of the reasons why leaders don't think much
about office design is because it doesn't have an
immediate short-term effect on productivity or revenue. But, like brushing your teeth, long-term habits
pay off over time. You'd have to stop brushing your
teeth for a long time before some of your teeth fell out.
But they would. Similarly, companies may not see an

immediate link between improving their office design and culture. But be patient. Over time, it will become apparent.

The initial cost of redesigning an office space can be a bit daunting (I'll share some money-saving tips to help with this). But keep in mind that there'll be benefits, tangible and intangible, that are worth every penny. When companies ask themselves, 'What are the long-term behaviours that we know will drive our economic success?' and then design their office space around that, the transformation and benefits are incredible.

In fact, our leadership team at Peer 1 Hosting had discussions with staff about working remotely from home. But the vast majority of people didn't want to work from home because they were having so much fun in the office. They were pleased with their productivity, which they knew derived from the unique working environment. We'd created such a comfortable and collaborative environment that people loved coming to work and were incredibly productive.[75] When prospective clients and interview candidates visited us, they said, 'Wow!' and wanted to work with us or for us.

Many companies have moved to a hybrid model of working, with staff working in the office part time and working the rest of their hours at home. The premise here is nevertheless the same: your office space needs to be designed with the end goal in mind. How do you create a space that's better than home or Starbucks for your employee to carry out their role and achieve their aims?

People don't come to work to do a poor job and be idle all day. They generally want to do meaningful work with other great people. And one way a company can encourage this natural behaviour is to provide an environment that's physically conducive to meaningful work, which means changing the layout of your office. Let's investigate some ways you can do this.

Quick and easy ways to change your office setup

Integrate monitors everywhere

Later, we'll dig into some more significant changes you can make, but a simple one is to add monitors with metrics around your office space. Put monitors up all over your organisation so that everyone can see team scores, company scores and other essential statistics. It keeps people focused, reveals what you value, and how you're fulfilling your mission.

At Peer 1 Hosting, we put up monitors that showed daily and weekly metrics that teams were responsible for and shared them throughout the company. Focusing on lagging indicators is like driving your car while looking through the rearview mirror, so we didn't just post lagging indicators, but also leading indicators. Posting these 'scores' built a sense of cama- raderie and reminded people how various teams were working together to achieve certain goals.

Details about upcoming demonstrations, conferences, meetings and proposals that will lead to future sales also need to be displayed, showing employees what's coming up and what they are working towards.

Create different spaces for different kinds of work

I'm a big proponent of open office spaces. Some peo- ple object to open office spaces because they claim it inhibits deep work. But you can design different kinds of spaces for different types of work. Create quiet spaces, socialising areas, places where teams can meet. At Peer 1 Hosting, we created a library, and people just knew to whisper in there and stay off their phones.

We instinctively know that in specific environments, certain behaviours are expected. No one tells you to whisper in a church or a library, but you usually do. Behaviours are inherent to the environment people inhabit, so it's best to ask, 'What are the behaviours that my team default to in different types of environ- ments in our office?' Then design your office based on that.

Some office spaces make you feel claustrophobic. The leaders cram as many cubicles as they can into a room and think that is ideal, or that more desks mean more output. But people don't want to work in places like that. They want to have a variety of options to choose from for the different kinds of activities that fill their day. When you create various spaces for diverse functions, people will naturally gravitate to the room that best facilitates their needs.

How you label rooms can also help your office reflect company culture. We had a training room, but we didn't call it a training room. We called it the cinema room. We added a popcorn machine and bought chairs for it from a local cinema that was doing a refurbishment. The staff would have a film night there once a week, but we typically used it for team meetings. If we had called it the training room, no one would have used it for socialising.

If you design the room as a cinema, you can also use it as a training room. But if you design the space as a training room, it becomes a stuffy corporate room with no other purpose. By buying second-hand cinema seats, we saved a considerable amount of money compared to how much it would've cost to create a training room. Who says you have to buy office furniture? Be creative.

After we finished designing our new office space for Peer 1 Hosting, we had camera crews from all over

Europe reporting on the uniqueness of our space. Reporters said that we had the 'coolest' office in Britain outside of Google.[76] We had only spent about £25 per square foot, yet the office was incredibly modern, fun, creative, warm, homey, whimsical, inviting and multifunctional. We even had our own pub.

A major global oil company had its office designed by the same firm we worked with, and they spent three times the amount per square foot for a bland office space. We spent one-third less but were getting covered on the nightly news while they ended up with a vanilla template office that no one noticed. But more than that, our office space created an environment where we did incredible work and forged new partnerships, partnerships that developed because of the culture people saw in and around the office.

Input from your team is vital

As I've mentioned before, I pre-approve projects. I set the criteria and then let a team create the proposal or report. This ensures that the team owns the outcome and assumes the burden of responsibility for it. Instead of me telling them to cut this or that to make budget, they must make those decisions themselves. It forces them to prioritise and saves me from being the person they're frustrated with for saying 'no'.

Once, when a company I was working for was preparing to move into a new office, I surveyed my team to learn what they liked about the existing space, what they didn't like, and the changes they'd like to see in the future. I also sent the entire staff a link to a website that had pictures of innovative office spaces to get the creative juices flowing. Some people wanted a climbing wall, others wanted a herb garden, but the team was in charge of designing the space. It's not my place as a CEO to get into the weeds about those things. I asked for a volunteer to manage the design committee and to focus on the details so that I could concentrate on our mission and vision.

The committee decided to convert one room into a pub and put in a full bar. Now in Peer 1 Hosting offices all around the world, four o'clock on Friday is beer o'clock. I personally wasn't in favour of a bar, but the committee was passionate about it. They even made sure that the pub had nuts and crisps each week and had an opening celebration to stock the bar with people's unwanted bottles from home, which we turned into cocktails.

This kind of grassroots planning is better than a top-down dictum because the staff know what they want for themselves better than I do. We learned what kind of spaces people wanted and the variety of environments that would enhance productivity and team building, and we developed creative suggestions into workable solutions.

Wow your guests with something unique

We put the meeting rooms upstairs, and a bright yellow helter-skelter slide from that level down to the entrance area. When guests arrived, I'd slide down to greet them. Ta-da! It was an unforgettable moment for them. As soon as people walked into the office, you could see by their facial expression that they were thinking, 'There's something different about this company.'

We also decided not to hire a receptionist so that each employee could walk our guest through the office to show them what we're all about. The company had electronic registration and rotated staff near the front door, so the whole workforce was invested in welcoming clients. All employees had to learn the office tour. It was in the shape of a figure eight downstairs and upstairs, and took people via different artefacts to tell them our story.

We created a script, and during the onboarding process, new employees would memorise it. Then they would give the tour to their team, and the team would provide brutally honest feedback about the presentation. Over time, the whole office gave exceptional presentations, and I'm certain that greeting a new client in this way led to meaningful partnerships and to top-tier hires.

In the next section, I'll take you on a sample tour. You'll learn about my philosophy behind the various choices we made and how they impacted company culture, efficiency and success.

A cultural tour with a difference

From reception, an employee would greet the visitor and ask, 'Would it be all right if I gave you a tour of the office? Dominic is upstairs in the meeting room, but we'd like to take you around the office, get you a cup of coffee, and show you a bit about our company before you get started.' The employee (let's say Joe) would then take the new client (let's say Tina) to our 'brag wall', where she'd see some of the great companies we work with. Then Joe would take Tina to a monitoring wall, where she'd see that Peer 1 hosts 1% of the entire internet. Next, Tina would see our network monitoring centre, where she'd view a team busily working at their standing desks.

After that, Joe would show Tina our travel wall with postcards pinned to a map, written from employees to their colleagues on holiday. Tina would then see a wall filled with documents and photographs from new employees who had completed a 'Ten Things You Don't Know About Me' form. We share this with the organisation before new people start so that the other employees feel a connection with new hires and have some conversation openers in mind for when they meet. Joe would then show Tina our core values poster and a wall filled with Post-it notes supporting these values. This was where the team posted about employees who were caught doing the right thing by their colleagues.

Tina would even see the 'Cock-up of the Month', where the biggest mistake made was posted so that people could learn from the mistakes and realise that we have a culture of forgiveness. If things are swept under the carpet, you never make progress. We can learn just as much from our failures as we can from our successes. So we put them on the wall and celebrated them.

Next, Joe and Tina would arrive at our tree of gratitude, where people could write notes and pin them to the tree, giving thanks for a particular co-worker. The employee with the most notes would become the employee of the month.

We also used a 120-degree desk arrangement, because it's more organic than straight lines and creates a warmer environment. There were no pedestals for people to store their things in. Instead, we had lockers so that an employee could grab his laptop and work in any number of different environments (and log in to any phone).

We even put in a pitch and putt so that employees could take a break and have some fun. Various studies show that a short break every hour enhances productivity. Why not do something fun during that time? Later we added a pool table, dartboard and table football because we knew this would foster friendships and facilitate a better sense of community and teamwork. Side note: one client asked about the rules. 'When can your employees play pool? What if someone wants to play all day? What if too many people want to play at the same time?' I told him that each team makes up their own rules. A support team could play pool for fifteen minutes if there weren't any calls in the queue. Another team may have a different rule. Management never policed it and never felt a need to do so.

We used outdoor furniture in our design, a) because it was cheap and b) so that each room had a *very* different feel, enabling employees to work and gather in a variety of environments. We also posted core values throughout the various rooms to reinforce our culture. Tina would see monitors throughout the building that shared key metrics.

Our team repurposed some kitchen furniture from the restaurant that had occupied the site before us and we created coffee pods on each floor, complete with an industrial coffee machine for those who wanted a nice hot cappuccino or macchiato. Teams could also meet on tiered wooden bleachers that felt like a sauna space. There were plenty of meeting spaces of various sizes, suitable for one-to-ones or for ten or twenty people to meet, and areas for people to work privately. We even put in swings so that people could chat and swing at the same time. Why not? It's fun, and it's even possible that this kind of movement enhances brainstorming compared to remaining sedentary.

Since every employee needs to lead the tour at one point or another, they slowly absorb the company's history, mission, vision and values and take ownership of it. Plus, by the time the visitor arrives in the meeting room, there's no need for me to give a company presentation. A staff member has already shared our corporate history, successes, purpose, mission, values, whom we serve, what we do and how we do it, so Tina doesn't need to endure a long PowerPoint presentation from me. And it comes across so much better when an employee does this rather than me.

Instead of the information sounding like I'm making a sales pitch, they hear about the company from a motivated employee, and it's a genuine description of who we are and what we do. It feels more natural or organic to hear a story and to walk around the office seeing people in action and viewing various stations than listening to a presentation in a meeting room. It's like the difference between reading about Italy and visiting Italy.

Finally, because we wanted to leave the visitor with a great memory, Tina would leave by going down the slide. The last thing she remembers about Peer

1 Hosting is, 'Yee-haw!' When visitors go down the slide, they feel a sense of euphoria or of being a small child again. They know this is a fun place to work, and that's their enduring memory of being in our office.

Now you can see how your office design can convey your company culture. It can also enhance your work-flow. At the offices of a major automotive brand's leasing arm in the United Kingdom, leaders looked at the physical journey that certain paperwork went on and then sat people next to one another based on that process. Prior to that, these people were scattered throughout the building. Now the person next to you would be the person handling that piece of paper before it's your turn.

If everything was done electronically, and 10% of the time there was a problem with the process, you'd likely be hesitant to email your co-worker about the concern. But, if your co-worker (that you just had tea with) is sitting right next to you, when an issue arises, you can immediately lean over and say, 'Mike, each time you do that, it makes my job harder. Can you do that differently to save me the headache?'

Internal health leads to external health

At several companies I've worked at, every quarter we would change the desk arrangement so that people from different departments could sit together. But we could only do this because of the open office design we'd created. We would easily rotate seating plans, and it solved many problems. For instance, there was a woman that didn't like one of our developers. She thought he was lazy, incompetent and rude. I had her sit with him, and after a month she came to me and apologised for having assumed the worst about him. She shared that she now thought he was fantastic. This rotation also created awareness and cross-pollination of knowledge, which helped our company flourish.

Cross-functional, rotating teams, rather than 'silos' of marketing, finance, or sales, for example, have proven to be a key to our success. But you need to create an office space where these kinds of variations can be implemented. There has to be a physical manifestation of your mission, vision and values in your office space so that it's conducive to the kind of work and culture you desire.

To better serve customers, build relationships in the organisation so that employees love the company. The reason is simple: your customers will never love your firm if your team doesn't. And one way they can fall in love with your company is by building an office space that facilitates healthy working relationships. Your external service can never be better than your internal service. The internal service has to be better than the external service, and a good office design can enhance both.

My goal was to make Peer 1 Hosting the number-one employer of choice in our region. Redesigning the office space was part of what led us to achieve that goal because it created the environment for meaningful, creative and diverse relationships and work. Within a minute of walking around the office, prospective clients or potential employees felt the energy of the place and wanted to be a part of what we were doing. Some people said it was like a beehive, and you could 'hear' the buzz.

When people walk into your office, do they want to work there because it's a great place to hang out, or does it feel like a typical dreary office? Make sure your premises reflect your company culture, and you'll see how this can revolutionise your organisation.

Summary

- Your office space should reflect your company culture. It has to facilitate your employees' best work, offering functional purpose and creative opportunity. An office space that doesn't work for them doesn't work for your business. It has to work better for them than their homes or Starbucks.

- Don't be put off by the initial cost of revamping your office – it will repay you in so many ways in the long-term.

- Use your fixtures, fittings and furnishings to your advantage – fit screens so that your teams can always see their key stats. Furnish the place creatively so that there are spaces for teams to work together and places for individuals to work alone as needed.

- When thinking about a redesign, ask your team members for their input. They will tell you what they want – and you don't have to agree with what is right for them, you just need to listen. If you cater to their wishes, they'll be motivated to do their best work in that environment.

- Your design doesn't need to be fixed. Rotating the desks every so often can lead to new relationships forming or old relationships improving. Get your team members talking to one another. They may surprise themselves with how effective this is. Remember, happy teams make happy customers.

9

Most Meetings Are Shit

Meetings are an insight into a company's culture. When hired as a business coach, I ask the CEO to share what they think the company's problems are. Then, to check whether they're correct or whether the problem is somewhere else, all I have to do is attend a meeting. In the 'micro' of a meeting, you see the 'macro' of the problem. Meetings are where company culture and execution come together, so if I see a problem in meetings, I know it's an indication of a company-wide issue.

Culture is how people behave when no one is looking, and it's the unwritten rules of acceptable behaviours in a company. Are people on time? Do people prepare? Do people listen to one another? Are they focused on making progress? Most of the attributes you desire to see in a successful business should be seen in company meetings. (And if they're lacking in a meeting, they're probably lacking in the business.)

And since no company outperforms its leadership team, how the leadership team conducts their meetings will set the tone for the rest of the organisation. If you're the CEO and the leadership team is your team, the way you run your team meetings is how you're running the company. It's the culture that you've set. Your meetings are typically a mirror of your leadership style and the culture you've created.

If you want to change the company's culture, one of the best places to start is in your meetings. Ask yourself, 'What kind of business do we want to be?' As soon as you know the answer to that, ask yourself, 'What type of meetings do we need to become that business?' To be blunt, if you don't have effective and engaging meetings, the business at large will never change.

Make meetings purposeful

Business meetings should be about solving big problems and making hard decisions. Yet often meetings squander time and add little value to the company or employees. Most companies would thrive if they cut some of their meetings. If you treat time as an asset, then you should only schedule essential meetings.

A meeting must have context and purpose. If those aren't clear, cancel it. If you invite people to a meeting, it should be obvious why you're taking up their precious time. If you receive an invitation to a meeting, the reason for the meeting and the desired outcome should be crystal clear. Empower your employees by telling them that if a meeting request has no clear context or desired outcome, they don't have to attend it.

Meetings are often used to communicate when communication could've been accomplished through an email or a video. Don't use meetings to just communicate. Getting thirty people in a room to announce something is talking. That's not a meeting. The value of a meeting is in bringing people together to brainstorm, to prioritise a problem or opportunity, and to gather input to make smart decisions.

Meetings usually have the wrong combination of people attending. Think carefully about who needs to be in a given meeting and why. Usually, you don't need more than seven people in the room. More than this and the meeting slows down, resulting in poorer decisions.

What if your meetings were optional?

Ask your people, 'What does a great meeting look like?' After listening to their response, ask, 'How many meetings do you attend that look like that?' It's likely that only a small percentage of their meetings look like their ideal meeting because most meetings are shit.

Tell your teams to find ways to cut superfluous meetings or reinvent the current ones to be effective, inspirational, productive and worthwhile. Reducing meetings (ie trimming useless fat) may be the best thing for your company.

Employees who are in endless meetings never get any work done. Or they're answering emails during the meeting and are totally zoned out. If employees feel they have to do other work in meetings, then they're in too many meetings. I once consulted with a business that had a few employees who were in back-to-back meetings four days a week. They complained that they couldn't get any of their work done nor meet their KPIs. We freed these employees from needless meetings, and their productivity skyrocketed.

Most meetings can be shorter. If you stay focused, you can probably accomplish what's done in a one-hour meeting in thirty minutes. Wasting time in unnecessary meetings causes tremendous opportunity cost. What your employees could accomplish if they weren't in meetings could be a game-changer for your company. Trim the fat and let them focus on the meat.

A great exercise that you can do in your company is to make all meetings optional. If you do this for a while, you'll learn a lot about your company. Which individuals attend nearly all optional meetings? Which individuals very rarely attend any optional meetings? Which meetings continue because people want to attend them, and they're useful? Which meetings drop off because nobody wants to attend them or because they're useless? The cream will rise to the top. Unproductive meetings will disappear and what you thought was essential will be exposed as pointless, or is easily replaced with an email, document, or video.

In a meeting, we have to debate, disagree, say our piece and then commit.[77] When we leave a meeting, we can't bitch and moan. Once the meeting is over, we must support the agreed-upon decision. Otherwise, you're acting like a small child, not an adult. Gossiping, divisive complaining, manoeuvring, scheming, dissenting and conspiring have no place in a healthy business. People are free to continue a debate and raise objections in subsequent meetings. But continued triangulation should be forbidden and enforced with the penalty of termination.

Get the right chair

I've observed that meetings tend to be chaired by the most senior person in the room. Most leaders think that they must run the meeting. But if that's not your strength, let someone else do it. Find someone skilled at running meetings and let them facilitate.

I'm crap at running meetings. I don't follow the rules. I go off on tangents. Most importantly, I won't change, so I always get someone else to run meetings. Problem solved!

Many senior leaders are not the most skilled in running meetings, so give it up and let someone else do it. Again, ask the staff what great meetings would look like, and then design the meetings based on their input.

Key roles in business meetings

Each meeting needs a facilitator, a timekeeper, and a notetaker. Let's look at these in turn.

The facilitator

The facilitator ensures that the meeting follows the framework or agenda. They keep everyone on target and focused on the desired outcome of the meeting. They also refuse to put any other business (AOB, which also stands for all other bollocks) on the agenda. I want to take the person who puts AOB on the agenda and kick them in the shins (not really, but the impulse is there). Never allow AOBs – they drain time and cause people to babble on about anything and everything. And try not to assault anyone either!

When I'm a facilitator, I use what's called a Level 10 Meeting template, which Gino Wickman wrote about in his book *Traction: Get a grip on your business.*[78] We begin with personal check-ins, when each person can share briefly about a win or an 'aha!' moment. This sets a positive tone for the meeting and ensures that everyone has an opportunity to speak. One of the main gripes about meetings is that 85% of the time is spent listening to two or three people talking. The extroverts in the room never get bored with listening to themselves. And they don't listen when they stop talking. They think about what smart thing they can say when the other person stops speaking. With this template, every person gets an equal amount of airtime for this segment (two minutes) and feels that they're contributing and have been heard.

Then we do a scorecard review that uses traffic light colours:

- Green = all good, on track, or completed

- Amber = warning or attention required

- Red = major problems or management action required

We check on our KPIs (key performance indicators) and OKRs (objectives and key results) and make sure none of the items are red or off track. We ask if any of the red items need to go on the agenda, and then we prioritise them. We're mainly looking for anything urgent, a big red flag that we must discuss. Once they're prioritised, we know what we must talk about first and don't waste time talking about other items. This prevents us from waiting until the end to talk about what's critical.

We then discuss employee and client feedback that people on the team can learn from or celebrate. Next, we review our to-do list to make sure that we check off what has been completed, review what hasn't been done, and discuss what's in progress. All of these aforementioned sections are under five minutes long. For the bulk of the meeting, we cover IDS, which stands for identify, discuss and solve. Prior to this, we've been giving context. Now, we focus on identifying problems and discussing how to solve them. Again, we vote on the top priorities and discuss them based on an agreed-upon prioritisation.

We don't try to rush into a quick fix. Instead, we want to brainstorm several ways to tackle the problem and then agree upon the best solution. Next, we put accountability measures in place so that nothing falls through the cracks. For that, you need the three Ws:

- Who is doing the task
- What the task is
- When it's going to be done by

We then take a few minutes to wrap up, review the to-do list, and plan the next steps for subsequent meetings. At the conclusion of a meeting, I add another step: participants rate the meeting on a scale of one to ten. This is about building culture. We're asking people about how they feel about this use of ninety minutes of their day. The feedback is about the process and not the people, so this allows people to be more transparent about their opinion.

Some will say the meeting was a seven, so I'll ask them, 'What could we have done differently to make this meeting a nine or a ten?' Sometimes I'll challenge people who gave a low score and say, 'Why didn't you speak up earlier about this?' I don't want to discourage people from sharing feedback, but I want them to see that they have a role in improving meetings. If Elliot rated the meeting as a 'three' and didn't participate, this may reveal that he doesn't need to be in the meeting anymore. Maybe it's a waste of his time and doesn't pertain to his area of responsibility or strengths.

The timekeeper

The timekeeper ensures that people don't talk too long and that other people have an opportunity to chime in. In my meetings, I give the timekeeper a yellow card and a red card, like a football referee. If the timekeeper holds up the yellow card, it means that the speaker needs to finish. Others in the room can say, 'No, what he's saying is important. Give him a few more minutes,' but the yellow card is a warning. The timekeeper needs to have the moral fortitude to be strict and can't be a pushover.

The timekeeper also makes sure that we start on time and finish on time. They use the red card to let someone know that their time is up, or to end the meeting. If the facilitator says, 'Let's talk about agenda item number three. We'd like to hear from Janet for five minutes,' the timekeeper sets their countdown timer on their smartphone and is ready with the yellow card (yes, they're allowed to use their phone).

The timekeeper could use the yellow card at the three-minute mark to indicate that people are bored and the same points are being repeated, so it's time to move on. The red card means that the agreed-upon time is up, and it's time to talk about something else or allow someone else to speak. Note, anyone can show a yellow card to indicate they feel we should move on, but the team decides to do so as a group.

The notetaker

I also have someone take notes in real-time in Google Docs. Detailed minutes are too long, and no one reads them. I want the notetaker to capture the agenda items, what we worked through, what decisions were made and who is responsible for action items (a clear statement about *who* will do *what* by *when* and what 'done' looks like).

The notes are about accountability, not transcription. This is why I don't want everyone in the room taking their own notes on their laptops. I want one person to capture the agreed-upon decisions and action items that have emerged from that meeting. They can all see this one version in a Google Doc. Everyone is on the same page, literally. You can even allow various people to edit the doc later if they feel that something was miscommunicated or needs clarification, as the changes are tracked. Or the person could post a comment that needs approval by the facilitator or notetaker.

You could also consider recording all of your Zoom meetings. There's no reason why most meetings couldn't be recorded using a simple audio recorder. In his book *Principles: Life and work,* Ray Dalio states that his company records all of their meetings and posts them on their server so that any employee can listen to the meetings.[79] The leadership wants to be transparent in what they do, and they want people to be able to go back and reference a meeting if they missed it or need to refresh their memories.

When in meetings, also tell people to put their phones and laptops away so that they can concentrate. No need to take notes. No temptation to check email or social media on your phone. You can start the meeting with a statement like this: 'Put everything away. This meeting is being recorded, so you can review any part of it afterwards. A summary of the meeting will be posted in a Google Doc. Let's get to work.'

If you're not using a gifted facilitator, timekeeper and notetaker, you're missing out on key people who can help your meetings run smoothly and productively.

Different kinds of meetings

Companies benefit from implementing an array of meetings. One type teams should have is a daily huddle or daily standup. This could consist of a front-line team huddle, a management team huddle and an executive team huddle, cascading up the organisation. These ten to fifteen minutes in the morning save people hours throughout the day because it lets them know whether they're focusing on and prioritising the right things.

During the huddle, the team members talk about what they accomplished the day before and what objectives and outcomes they'll achieve today. I don't want to hear about their diary or calendar and all the meetings they have scheduled. I want to know what they're going to do to reach a specific metric and what they're doing to impact the company significantly. They might also share how someone helped them, but that's it – two minutes max each.

Daily huddles enable people to say throughout the day, 'I appreciate this email and that post in Slack, but let's push them off to the morning huddle.' Gradually, employees learn what to talk about in the huddle and minimise unnecessary clutter in various chains of communication for the rest of the day. The team manager doesn't need to facilitate the daily huddle. You can rotate who leads it each day.

Weekly management meetings, quarterly strategy reviews and a theme for each quarter or year are also important. Themes are great for staying on target and can be depicted using various charts or progress indicators. I've personally seen how a quarterly theme can catalyse an organisation. I had always thought that themes were nice and helpful, but when I was hired at itlab and we only had a quarter to revive the business, I learned how critical themes could be. The theme we developed kept us all laser-focused on moving from point A to point B and saved the business.

If you know what the most important thing to fix is, base your quarterly theme on that. This will also help you know what to emphasise in various meetings – you tie the meeting priorities to the theme.

Don't waste your meetings

Think through your meetings. See them as a crucial strategy for creating culture and building your business.

Next time you're on a retreat with your senior leaders, consider kick-starting it with a brainstorming session about the current status of meetings, what needs to change, what an ideal rhythm of meetings would look like, how they're connected to your culture and how the meetings should be run. Implement your decisions for the rest of the retreat, and continue honing them after you get back.

Don't squander the power of meetings. Use them to develop people, create culture, focus your organisation and accelerate greater levels of success.

Summary

- Meetings are an insight into the company at large. Want to know a company's problems? Go to one of their meetings. Whatever your business culture is, it's what's happening in your leadership team meetings. They *are* the business after all.

- Most meetings are shit. End of. They are mostly a waste of time. If your meeting doesn't have a context or a purpose, cancel it.

- A radical, effective change you can implement in your company straight away is to make all meetings optional. You'll find out which meetings are vital and which ones can be cancelled for good. You'll also find out which employees are attending too many meetings or too few.

- What happens in the meeting stays in the meeting. There's no gossiping or moaning afterwards. Remember, meetings are micro examples of your company culture. Enforce the values you want for your company onto how meetings are conducted.

- Assign the key roles of chair, facilitator, timekeeper and notetaker to keep your meetings on track and to make the best use of the time. The most senior person may not make the best chair. The most junior person may not make the best notetaker.

- As always, think creatively. Do you need typed-up notes or could you use an audio recording? Perhaps you just want to record the meeting objectives. Do you need a meeting around a table or could you have a quick team huddle?

- Use a variety of meeting types and frequencies to satisfy different business needs: a daily huddle, a weekly check-in, a quarterly strategy review, etc.

- Having a meeting strategy is a winning tool in your business toolkit. Get strategic about meetings, and business strategy itself will improve.

10
Make Your Values Matter

People often talk about hard skills and soft skills. A hard skill could be your project management skills or Photoshop skills. A soft skill could be emotional intelligence. A company's values are often focused on soft skills – fluffy, mushy ideas that don't really translate into anything tangible. It's great to want people to be kind, helpful, hard-working and loyal, but those are values that focus on virtues rather than action. Virtues are essential and can drive actions, or cause actions to be done in the right way, but the values I'm after are what makes a company unique and enables them to accomplish their BHAG™. You could call them hard values.

You can be kind, hard-working and loyal in just about any industry. Those values are helpful whether you're a nurse, teacher, salesperson, musician or athlete. But your corporate values need to be specific traits that make or break your business. The mindset I'm after says, 'If my employees don't embody *these* values, my company will never get noticed, or it will fail.'

Nearly every company says they value integrity, teamwork and excellence. So what? Who doesn't? What company would say, 'We value corruption, dickheads and shoddy work'? None! So, don't put up generic, vanilla terms on your wall that mean nothing.

Values show how you approach positive or negative behaviours. Let people know what behaviours you'll celebrate and what you won't tolerate. Don't copy and paste the values and behaviours of other companies. And don't assume those generic values are motivational or inspiring. Your values must reflect the current company culture and how you want people to behave. They must stand out.

Avoid aspirational values that sound like something out of a Disney film. Think deeply about who you are, what you do, and how you do it as a company, and then work from there. Values can't merely be what you hope to become. That can be part of your mission. Values are the non-negotiable aspects of your company that foster growth. Your purpose explains why your company does what it does. Your values reveal *how* you do it.

How to live your values

The real question is, 'How do we get our staff to live out our values?' That's the crux of the matter. When a company is small, with, say, six employees, it's easy to set the culture. Everyone knows what everyone else is doing, and this small team usually has similarities or common values, which is why they started the business together in the first place. But as the company grows and you have thirty-five employees, a different culture will develop. If you're not intentional about setting the culture, you'll be stuck with a monster.

At one company I worked at, we came up with several values. Two of them were 'obsession' and 'smart'. Below you can see the behaviours we listed which corresponded to the given value:

Value: Obsession

Behaviour	Description
Demonstrates a customer service focus	• Looks at everything from the customer's perspective • Explains technical concepts clearly to the customer, avoiding technical jargon

Continued

Behaviour	Description
Commercial awareness	• Understands the resources and costs associated with delivering services • Always questions whether our company will benefit from work performed • Promotes our company professionally in all customer interactions
Demonstrates pride in work	• Displays pride and integrity in personal contribution

Value: Smart

Behaviour	Description
Takes initiative	• Takes the initiative in getting things done and improving things • Always looks for ways to improve customer service and the client network
Enthusiastically supports change	• Actively participates in contributing to change • Shows a willingness to adapt to enable the business to succeed • Takes responsibility for understanding the need for change, seeking support where necessary • Encourages others to be positive about change
Organises and plans work	• Organises time and information effectively • Develops and uses effective plans

We asked employees to rate themselves using the following grades.

- Grade F: Unacceptable

- Grade C: Improvement needed

- Grade B: Competent

- Grade A: Strong

- Grade A+: Role Model

Additionally, we asked a fellow team member (or team leader) to rate other team members. They, too, used the above rating scale.

Once the employees had rated themselves, they would share their grades with their teammates, before discussing them with their team leader or manager. Employees often have blind spots. This activity enabled them to get feedback on their behaviours – like a highly structured version of the stop/start/continue exercise we looked at earlier. Without a behavioural framework against which to measure culture, you can only measure performance, which leads to toxic A-players being tolerated.

If you do the above exercise in your company, the results will be illuminating, and you'll have some recruitment decisions to make. Your corporate values should be used to hire, fire, develop and promote people. The right values attract the right people, whether customers or employees. If the values are clear and aren't generic, they'll turn some people off, but will be a magnet for other people who can advance the company. It's best to include these values in your job ads so that the company culture is crystal clear to potential employees.

At Rackspace, we wanted to improve customer communication. We started reminding people that we valued verbal communication (eg phone calls) over written communication (eg emails, support tickets). We knew that customers were frustrated with other companies who only responded via emails and ticketing systems. We knew that we wanted to differentiate ourselves from our competitors by making our teams available and responsive over the phone.

Over time, when managers interviewed new hires, they'd intuitively ask, 'How good are you on the phone? How many times do you speak to customers over the phone each week?' Because the value was clear, interviewers knew how to sniff out people who just wouldn't cut it on their team, and they stopped hiring people who were phone shy.

Who are your clones?

If you can't define the minimum standards of behaviour for your organisation, anything goes. With that idea in mind, I often ask my clients, 'Can you name the five employees you'd like to clone?' Or I'll ask a question that Jim Collins came up with: 'If you were tasked with starting a new division of your business on Mars, which five employees from your company would you send?'[80]

I then ask the client to list the behaviours these five people exhibit day in and day out that they admire and value. We then cluster those behaviours and write a value that is an overarching theme for them. Then we'll highlight two or three behaviours that exemplify each value. These could be synthesised from the previously listed behaviours or could be taken directly from that list.

After this exercise, the leaders have a clear picture of the ideal employee. They have a clear picture of behaviours that they'll reward and behaviours that are out of order. What also emerges from this exercise are the unique values that drive this company. When that happens, the questions change to: 'What do we do with this? How do we inculcate all of this, look for examples of embodied values and reward this behaviour? How will we communicate these values to our company?'

During this exercise, we ask for stories that illustrate each value, something an employee did that exemplified this ideal behaviour. The stories create emotional buy-in. If a leader can share a testimony about a wonderful thing Sarah did and how it made them feel, it

MIND YOUR F**KING BUSINESS

helps others connect to that value. Celebrate successes like Sarah's at weekly meetings, and you'll soon be building and sharing a cultural DNA.

How many times have you celebrated employees who embodied your values? After telling the staff a heart-warming story about one employee's hard work and dedication, I gave a bottle of champagne to this employee because he exemplified a particular value. Allow other employees to speak about how a co-worker helped them and demonstrated a value to share and spread this approach.

One company I worked with solicits employee feedback each month. It then gives a reward to the employee who received the most compliments based on specific company values. Co-workers must list which value their colleague displayed in their praise. In a short amount of time, people want to behave according to the company values because they know this brings recognition and rewards. I call this social capital. Before you know it, that behaviour comes more naturally to the employees, and the values are embodied.

Celebrate the things you want your employees to do more of. Find ways to applaud the behaviours that exemplify your values, and your employees will gradually begin to form a culture that aligns with them. Otherwise, the values on the wall will get lost, and you'll turn into a 'grey' business in a heartbeat.

You'll be a beige, forgettable organisation if you don't relentlessly instil your values into your employees.

It's impossible to have happy customers without happy staff. Happy leadership and staff lead to happy customers, which leads to a profitable business. That's how you develop a high-performance team. But you can't have a high-performance team without having a minimum set of behaviours that employees agree upon and live by. That's where your values come in. They tell everyone what's expected, how business should be conducted and what will not be tolerated.

How do you embed values into your company?

When Amazon was starting out, new employees were given a cheap door and some trestle legs from The Home Depot, along with some screws and tools. The leadership wanted to communicate that frugality was a core value, so no desks were bought. Employees had to build their own.[81]

Amazon's leadership created a physical manifestation of a value and behaviour that they wanted to be embedded in their company. When you work to bring values to life in your company, you will find ways to create symbols and rituals that foster the development of these values. You must find creative ways to make your values a part of everyone's daily work life.

One company I worked with said that their value was 'striving for excellence'. I asked how the sales team was performing. I also asked, 'If you doubled your sales team, would you double your revenue?' The manager said, 'Hell no!' He then proceeded to give me all kinds of excuses as to why only 12% of the sales team were hitting their numbers.

The company and management had a value about excellence and results, but the culture tolerated low standards. I told them that they should change their value on the poster from 'striving for excellence', to 'mediocre at best' or 'mediocrity is easier'! Too many companies give lip service to lofty values, but never do anything to embed or enforce them. This company was too afraid of making difficult decisions, so they lived with the dissonance between their values and their employees' performance.

One of our values at Rackspace was 'Honesty: Bad news first, no surprises.' This meant that if we cocked something up, we told the customers about our mistake. Customers had never experienced this before. They were shocked and amazed when we rang them up and explained what had happened. The staff that came from competitors were used to lying to customers about their mistakes. They would blame some company we worked with, IT, or some broken part, but never admitted that there was human error. New staff would often bristle against this value and say to me, 'If I tell the customer the truth, they'll think I'm incompetent and won't trust me.' And I would tell them, 'They already know you're incompetent. If they looked at the logs, they could see your mistake. Now they just know that you're honest about it.'

People can easily revert to the old ways of doing things. If you don't set up systems and structures to instil your values into your employees, your company culture will dissipate. Suppose you don't have a strong management training programme and aren't developing leaders from within your company. In that case, you'll hire from outside and bring in poor values that can drastically change your organisation. New people will show up and behave as they always have, changing the culture you've set. New recruits, especially those in management positions, must learn your values and should not be hired in the first place if they don't display them. You not only have to work to inculcate positive values, but you'll need to also put effort into helping people unlearn opposing values or put more effort into hiring from within.

This may be too much of a generalisation, but people who play or have played team sports make great employees. They have a resilience to them and an understanding of how to function as a team. These people are used to turning up once or twice a week, rain or shine, for a game that most people in the world don't know about. They're not being paid to play, and they're not seeking glory for themselves. They play for the love of the game and to support their teammates.

People who play team sports are prepared to work hard and practise, and they have doggedness and grit. They get up early on Saturday to play, season in and season out, and keep going each year whether they win or lose. They've learned how to get along with others.

I've played rugby all my life, and there are always a few people on the team that you're not going to hang out with after the season ends, but whom you've learned to work well with. They're not on your Christmas card list, but you find a way to make things work, coalescing around an objective. Ideally, there are friends on the team that look out for one another, celebrate successes together and make the team tighter. But either way, the values you learn from playing a team sport translate to work and are worth exploring to communicate your expectations with your team more effectively. What do you see in your favourite sports team that could be a value for your work team?[82]

The sabotage exercise

One way to help your team brainstorm and agree upon shared behavioural standards is by running the sabotage exercise. I ask a team how they would sabotage their company from the inside if a competitor paid them to do it. They love this and soon begin to feel like they're in a James Bond film: 'We'd hire shitty people and encourage others not to turn up for meetings. We'd piss the clients off with horrible customer service so that contracts would be cancelled. We'd spread terrible rumours about the leaders, stoking fear in the employees and division all around.'

Then we ask the team if they see any of these behaviours in the company. Gradually, they begin to see that they don't need competitors to sabotage the company – they're doing it themselves by some of their actions. So, we then wordsmith ten behaviours that we'll no longer tolerate as a team. It could be, 'We no longer tolerate meetings that don't start on time.' Or, 'We will never fail to respond to an email.' The employees indirectly indict past behaviours that have frustrated them and then enshrine the opposite of those behaviours 'into law'. We typically write these in a positive way, such as, 'We will be punctual for meetings.' Or, 'We will respond promptly to emails.'

We then write a team charter based on these values and behaviours. Everybody signs it, and then we take a picture of the team signing the charter and post it on the wall in the conference room. You can post the text of the team charter on the wall as well. Then, whenever someone is out of line, you can point to the picture and say, 'You're doing what we agreed we wouldn't do, and this is the second time you've done so in the past two weeks. Come to the meeting prepared next time.' If they don't, everyone on the team understands that this person was reprimanded or fired because he or she wouldn't play by the team's rules.

Importantly, you can't just do this once with one team, then apply the results to all other teams in your company. Since various behaviours may not be universal, each team should undergo this exercise and create their own team charter. For instance, the behaviours in the sales team may be quite different from the behaviours in the human resources team.

The Leadership Maturity Matrix

For each company that I coach, my goal is for them to develop a values-based leadership framework or what I've called a Leadership Maturity Matrix. These are values and behaviours that become increasingly difficult as the role moves up the leadership chain. The executive team has a set of behaviours that are similar to the ones for employees, but the matrix holds the leadership to a higher level of accountability. They are the same behaviours, just done better as responsibility and seniority increase. This helps employees see how to develop and be promoted, and also holds the leaders to the highest standard. Employees assess themselves on the matrix, and their team members give them feedback as well.

In the left-hand column of the matrix, I list values. Then across the top, I list the following four roles: player, captain, coach and master. Generally, what's expected of a 'lower' role (eg player) isn't as stringent as what's expected of a 'higher' role (eg master).

The Leadership Maturity Matrix example

VALUE	BEHAVIOURS			
	Player	Captain	Coach	Master
Every customer interaction matters	Focuses on the customer as a person (not revenue)	Understands and anticipates customers' needs	Skilfully addresses customer challenges	Brings a strategic perspective to emerging customer needs (forward planning)
Enables others to succeed	Seeks feedback from peers and offers feedback to peers	Delivers development feedback to reports and team	Coaches individuals and team towards high performance	Constantly scans, identifies and eliminates organisational barriers to success
Strives for excellence	Focuses on results by creating individual performance and leadership goals	Focuses the team on results by creating shared goals, objectives and metrics for the team	Identifies and leverages cross-functional interdependencies to achieve results	Establishes stretch goals and provides strategic vision for the company as a whole
Sense of fun and play	Recognises and appreciates the work and efforts of co-workers	Celebrates team's successes and milestones	Recognises contribution of peers across the organisation	Creates a culture of recognition and celebration

When I use the Leadership Maturity Matrix with clients, I usually list between five and ten leadership values. The following example shows four leadership values:

When I evaluated myself on my very own matrix, I realised that although I was in a leadership position, my actions surrounding a 'sense of fun and play' were subpar (I was closer to the player level than the master level). I had to create a framework for myself that enabled me to foster a culture of recognition and celebration.

One of my Gallup Strengths is 'Achiever'. And because Achievers are so focused on tasks, results, productivity and company progress, we don't celebrate success and don't say 'thank you' often enough. I asked my team to find examples of people doing the right thing and then asked them to craft a note for me that I could send to these exemplary workers. As I became more aware of my shortcomings from the matrix I helped to formulate, I created a culture of recognition and celebration by harnessing the help of others to overcome my shortcomings. When people ask, 'What do I do with these values?', you do this. You create a matrix that allows your employees to see what's expected from them and how to grow. Nobody is a master of all the things you'll see in my example. There's always room for improvement.

Even just working through the matrix can be helpful. For instance, at one company I worked with, the senior leadership team shared a matrix of values they had created with the directors. We asked everyone in this meeting to write their names on a large poster board and to indicate whether they thought they were at the level of player, captain, coach or master for each value.

One chap placed himself as a master of them all. It was ludicrous! I knew he had to go. A week after observing his self-assessment, he was let go, because the leadership realised he had a warped self-awareness and had already shown a pattern of poor behaviour. Even if you genuinely feel you're a master of everything, you should be humble and wise enough to know that you don't broadcast that to everyone.

I encourage you to create your own Leadership Maturity Matrix so that your company understands and lives out the values and behaviours that lead to success. The matrix can be used to hire, fire, develop and promote people. Don't just leave your values on a piece of paper to collect dust. Make your values matter.

Remember, when it comes to values and behaviours, it's essential to communicate with your staff what sets your company apart, what differentiates your company from others and what traits are needed from employees for them to thrive.

Summary

- What are your company's values? Are they hard values? Are they values your employees can live by? If not, rethink them. You don't want generic, vanilla values, nor wishy-washy soft values. You need hard values that your employees can bring to their work every day.

- Your business values should be used to hire, fire, develop and promote people. Put them in your job ads. Get your managers asking about them in interviews. The right values attract the right people to your company.

- Your values are also your expectations of your employees' behaviour – the standards they should be displaying in their work. Use exercises such as the sabotage exercise or asking your team members who they would clone to get them thinking about the behaviours they should exhibit and the values they should embody.

- Embed your values into your company systems. Make them part of your recruitment process, your meeting process, your rewards process. Make them impossible for your employees to opt out of.

- Use the Leadership Maturity Matrix to identify what your values look like at every level of your company, which will give your employees something to always be working towards. Beware of the individual who thinks they are a master of everything – they won't be, and they may need to be let go.

- Your values demonstrate what sets you apart, what differentiates you from the competition and what ultimately is key to your success: think carefully about what they are and get your employees to live and breathe them so that your company can thrive.

Conclusion

L et me conclude with a fascinating fact that perfectly illustrates my point about entrenched beliefs. Almost twenty-five years since the Iron Curtain came down, red deer roaming the Czech–German border still baulk at crossing areas where electric fences once lay. Despite the creatures having no living memory of the fences, they still avoid the area, so powerful is their herd instinct.[83]

I hope what you've read in this book has encouraged you to avoid the same mentality. You've learned ways of doing things you might not have considered. You know talented people come along so infrequently, you need to get them into your business as quickly as possible, even if there's no immediate role available. You'll avoid declaring you're 'customer-focused' if you've no way to back this up and measure it. You'll have the confidence to say no to annual appraisals and yes to a decent set of core values that mean something. Your meetings will be better run and your offices fit for a positive, engaged culture.

You're starting to look at your business through a different lens. You know you can use my advice to rebuild your culture, become customer-obsessed and develop a high-performing leadership team. At last, you have some clarity on what your business does better than anyone else.

Above all else, you've recognised the need to question. And you've found the courage to challenge your assumptions and the curiosity to explore a different way forward.

References

1   P Attia, '#103: Looking back on the first 99 episodes: Strong
    convictions, loosely held', *The Peter Attia Drive* (6 April
    2020), https://peterattiamd.com/strong-convictions-
    loosely-held

2   M Goldsmith, *What Got You Here Won't Get You There*
    (Profile Books, 2008)

3   AA Zoltners, P Sinha and SE Lorimer, 'Wells Fargo and the
    slippery slope of sales incentives', *Harvard Business Review*
    (20 September 2016), https://hbr.org/2016/09/wells-fargo-
    and-the-slippery-slope-of-sales-incentives

4   For more on this idea, read Daniel H Pink, 'Forget carrots
    and sticks, they don't always work', *The Telegraph* (22
    May 2010), www.telegraph.co.uk/finance/yourbusiness/
    business-thinking/7752986/Forget-carrots-and-sticks-they-
    dont-always-work.html

5   Daniel H Pink, *Drive: The surprising truth about what
    motivates us* (Canongate Books, 2011); Jim Collins, *Good to
    Great: Why some companies make the leap... and others don't*
    (Random House Business, 2001); Justin Roff-Marsh, *The
    Machine: A radical approach to the design of the sales function*
    (Ballistix, 2019)

6   X Zhang and KM Bartol, 'Linking empowering leadership
    and employee creativity: the influence of psychological
    empowerment, intrinsic motivation, and creative process
    engagement,' *AMJ*, 53/1 (2010), 107–128, https://doi.
    org/10.5465/amj.2010.48037118

7   D Ariely, 'What's the value of a big bonus?', *The New
    York Times* (19 November 2008), https://nytimes.
    com/2008/11/20/opinion/20ariely.html

8   T Chamorro-Premuzic, 'Does money really affect
    motivation? A review of the research', *Harvard Business
    Review* (10 April 2013), https://hbr.org/2013/04/does-
    money-really-affect-motiv

9   D Ledingham, M Kovac and H Locke Simon, 'The new
    science of sales force productivity', *Harvard Business Review*
    (September 2006), https://hbr.org/2006/09/the-new-
    science-of-sales-force-productivity, accessed October 2022

10 DH Pink explores these motivators in *Drive* (2011) (see note
    5)

11 SW Martin, 'Is your sales organization good or great?',
    Harvard Business Review (25 February 2013), https://hbr.
    org/2013/02/is-your-sales-organization-goo; Ryan Fuller,
    'What makes great salespeople,' *Harvard Business Review*
    (8 July 2015), https://hbr.org/2015/07/what-makes-great-
    salespeople

12 SW Martin, 'A portrait of the overperforming salesperson',
    Harvard Business Review (20 June 2016), https://hbr.
    org/2016/06/a-portrait-of-the-overperforming-salesperson

13 SW Martin, *Heavy Hitter Sales Psychology: How to penetrate
    the C-level executive suite and convince company leaders to buy*
    (TILIS, 2009)

14 Jim Collins, *Good to Great*; Jim Collins, 'The Hedgehog
    Concept', Jimcollins.com (no date), www.jimcollins.com/
    concepts/the-hedgehog-concept.html

15 See Mark Kovac, 'When you need sales specialists, not sales
    generalists', *Harvard Business Review* (18 February 2016),
    https://hbr.org/2016/02/when-you-need-sales-specialists-
    not-sales-generalists

16 The Great Place to Work Institute awarded Rackspace 18th
    Best Place to Work UK 2006, 13th Best Place to Work UK
    2005, and Top 100 European Best Places to Work 2005. The
    Great Place to Work Institute named Peer 1 Hosting the
    11th Best Place to Work UK in 2014, the 19th Best Place

to Work UK in 2013, and the 16th Best Place to Work UK in 2012. Best Companies named Peer 1 Hosting the best company to work for in 2008, the second-best company to work for in 2009, and 'Very Good Company to Work For' in 2019. They named itlab the third best small IT company to work for in 2007 and an 'Outstanding Company to Work For' in 2016. They named Rackspace the 6th best small company to work for in 2006.

17 M Mankins and E Garton, *Time, Talent, Energy: Overcome organizational drag and unleash your team's productive power* (Harvard Business Review Press, 2017)

18 If you're not familiar with Net Promoter Scores (NPS), hang in there. I'll explain what they are later in the chapter. If you want to learn what its inventors (Bain & Company, Fred Reichheld, and Satmetrix Systems) have to say about NPS, visit their official website, NetPromoterSystem.com, or read Fred Reichheld, *The Ultimate Question 2.0: How Net Promoter companies thrive in a customer-driven world* (Harvard Business Review Press, 2011)

19 To learn more about NPS, read Frederick F Reichheld, 'The one number you need to grow', *Harvard Business Review* (December 2003), https://hbr.org/2003/12/the-one-number-you-need-to-grow. To learn more about churn versus profit, read Frederick F Reichheld and W Earl Sasser Jr, 'Zero defections: Quality comes to services', *Harvard Business Review* (September–October 1990), https://hbr.org/1990/09/zero-defections-quality-comes-to-services

20 Ibid

21 F Reichheld, 'The one number you need to grow'

22 A Grove, *Only the Paranoid Survive: How to exploit the crisis points that challenge every company* (Profile Books, 1998)

23 A Agassi, *OPEN: An autobiography* (Harper NonFiction, 2010)

24 V Harnish, *Mastering the Rockefeller Habits: What you must do to increase the value of your fast-growth firm* (Gazelles Publishing, 2002)

25 For more on David Tudehope and Macquarie Telecom Group, listen to my podcast episode with David: Dominic Monkhouse, 'How to improve customer experience with net promoter score', *The Melting Pot with Dominic Monkhouse* (12 January 2021), https://monkhouseandcompany.com/podcast/how-to-improve-customer-experience-with-net-promoter-score

26 'Dunning–Kruger effect', *Psychology Today* (no date), www.psychologytoday.com/gb/basics/dunning-kruger-effect

27 SB Badal, 'How entrepreneurial talent drives business success', Gallup (22 January 2015), https://gallup.com/builder/243482/entrepreneurial-talent-drives-business-success.aspx

28 BD Smart, *Topgrading: The proven hiring and promoting method that turbocharges company performance* (Penguin Random House, 2012)

29 'CliftonStrengths', Gallup (2022), https://gallup.com/cliftonstrengths/en/252137/home.aspx

30 M Murphy, *Hiring for Attitude: A revolutionary approach to recruiting and selecting people with both tremendous skills and superb attitude* (McGraw Hill, 2016)

31 M Zetlin, 'Google Automatically rejects most resumes for common mistakes you've probably made too', *Inc.* (9 April 2018), www.inc.com/minda-zetlin/google-resume-mistakes-laszlo-bock-job-hiring-employment.html

32 A Chamberlain, 'Does company culture pay off? Analyzing stock performance of "Best Places to Work" companies', Glassdoor (11 March 2015), https://glassdoor.com/research/does-company-culture-pay-off-analyzing-stock-performance-of-best-places-to-work-companies

33 A Chamberlain and D Zhao, 'The key to happy customers? Happy employees', *Harvard Business Review* (19 August 2019), https://hbr.org/2019/08/the-key-to-happy-customers-happy-employees

34 H Stewart, *The Happy Manifesto: Make your organization a great workplace* (Kogan Page, 2013)

35 J Schatz, '5 ways to improve employee engagement', Gallup (17 July 2022), https://gallup.com/workplace/231581/five-ways-improve-employee-engagement.aspx

36 T Connelly, 'Research: Half of lawyers suffer "Sunday night fear"', *Legal Cheek* (3 February 2020), https://legalcheek.com/2020/02/research-half-of-lawyers-suffer-sunday-night-fear

37 D Sims and G Jackson, 'A third of UK employees experience "Sunday Night Fear", according to survey', DJS Research (6 February 2020), https://djsresearch.co.uk/BusinessSupportMarketResearchInsightsAndFindings/article/A-third-of-UK-employees-experience-Sunday-Night-Fear-according-to-survey-04539

38 Best Companies and *The Sunday Times*, 'Best Companies league tables', Best Companies Ltd (no date), https://b.co.uk/league-tables

39 Fortune and Great Place to Work, '100 best companies to work for', Fortune Media (2022), https://fortune.com/best-companies/2022

40 'Best Places to Work 2022', Glassdoor (2022), https://glassdoor.com/Award/Best-Places-to-Work-LST_KQ0,19.htm

41 J Robison, 'In praise of praising your employees', Gallup (9 November 2006), https://gallup.com/workplace/236951/praise-praising-employees.aspx

42 'Gallup's employee engagement survey: Ask the right questions with the Q12 survey', Gallup (2022), https://gallup.com/workplace/356063/gallup-q12-employee-engagement-survey.aspx

43 https://www.happy.co.uk/'Join our movement to create joy at work', Happy Ltd (2022), https://happy.co.uk

44 'New survey reveals large regional differences in workers' commuting experience', *SME news* (13 September 2019), https://sme-news.co.uk/new-survey-reveals-large-regional-differences-in-workers-commuting-experience

45 M Buckingham and A Goodall, *Nine Lies About Work: A freethinking leader's guide to the real world* (Harvard Business Review Press, 2019)

46 O Jõgi, 'Reinventing performance management: A Deloitte case study', Business.com (1 September 2022), https://business.com/articles/reinventing-performance-management-a-deloitte-case-study

47 M Buckingham and A Goodall, 'Reinventing performance management', *Harvard Business Review* (April 2015), https://hbr.org/2015/04/reinventing-performance-management; M Buckingham and A Goodall, 'The feedback fallacy', *Harvard Business Review* (March–April 2019), https://hbr.org/2019/03/the-feedback-fallacy

48 M Buckingham and A Goodall, *Nine Lies About Work*

49 O Jõgi, 'Reinventing performance management'

50 J Doerr, *Measure What Matters: OKRs: The simple idea that drives 10x growth* (Penguin, 2018)

51 F Castro, 'What is OKR?', FelipeCastro.com (no date), https://felipecastro.com/en/okr/what-is-okr

52 For more on BHAGTM, see T Collins, *Good to Great*

53 F Castro, 'What is OKR?'

54 Bill Gates is quoted by J Kasperkevic in 'Bill Gates: Good feedback is the key to improvement', *Inc.* (17 May 2013), www.inc.com/jana-kasperkevic/bill-gates-proper-feedback-is-key-to-improvement.html

55 K Scott, *Radical Candor: How to get what you want by saying what you mean* (Macmillan, 2017)

56 E Batista, 'How to deliver critical feedback', EdBatista. com (19 July 2020), www.edbatista.com/2020/07/how-to-deliver-critical-feedback.html

57 A Sugihto, 'Dunbar's number: The rule of 150', Intention. al (1 December 2015), https://intention.al/blog/dunbars-number

58 AG Ingham et al, 'The Ringelmann effect: Studies of group size and group performance', *Journal of Experimental Social Psychology*, 10(4), pp371–384, www.sciencedirect.com/science/article/abs/pii/002210317490033X

59 M de Rond, 'Why less is more in teams,' *Harvard Business Review* (6 August 2012), https://hbr.org/2012/08/why-less-is-more-in-teams

60 J Morgan, 'Why smaller teams are better than larger ones', *Forbes* (15 April 2015), https://forbes.com/sites/jacobmorgan/2015/04/15/why-smaller-teams-are-better-than-larger-ones

61 SA Snook, *Friendly Fire: The accidental shootdown of US Black Hawks over northern Iraq* (Princeton University Press, 2002), p135

62 'The secret power of small teams: How to harness your potential', *Xero Blog* (no date), https://xero.com/blog/2017/04/secret-power-small-teams-workflowmax

63 D Wang and JA Evans, 'Research: When small teams are better than big ones', *Harvard Business Review* (21 February 2019), https://hbr.org/2019/02/research-when-small-teams-are-better-than-big-ones

64 Jeff Bezos quoted in 'Two-pizza teams', in M Mansoor et al, *Introduction to DevOps on AWS* (AWS White paper, Amazon Web Services, 2022), https://docs.aws.amazon.com/whitepapers/latest/introduction-devops-aws/two-pizza-teams.html

65 M Mankins and E Garton, 'How Spotify balances employee autonomy and accountability', *Harvard Business Review* (9 February 2007), https://hbr.org/2017/02/how-spotify-balances-employee-autonomy-and-accountability

66 Professor Moira Clark, Director of the Henley Centre for Customer Management (personal communication with the author, November 2022).

67 H Kniberg and A Ivarsson, 'Scaling Agile @ Spotify with tribes, squads, chapters and guilds' (white paper, October 2012), https://blog.crisp.se/wp-content/uploads/2012/11/SpotifyScaling.pdf

68 Nadya Powell, speaking at Silicon Beach (Bournemouth, 2017)

69 LJ Peter and R Hull, *The Peter Principle: Why things always go wrong* (Souvenir Press, 1994)

70 A Fleming, 'The key to adaptable companies is relentlessly developing people', *Harvard Business Review* (12 October 2016), https://hbr.org/2016/10/the-key-to-adaptable-companies-is-relentlessly-developing-people; S Sinek, 'Why good leaders make you feel safe', TED.com (2014), https://ted.com/talks/simon_sinek_why_good_leaders_make_you_feel_safe?language=en

71 The concept of a Tour of Duty is discussed in R Hoffman, B Casnocha and C Yeh, *The Alliance: Managing talent in the networked age* (Harvard Business Review Press, 2014)

72 Michael Bungay Stanier, *The Coaching Habit: Say less, ask more and change the way you lead forever* (Page Two, 2016)

73 Henry Stewart, *The Happy Manifesto*

74 R Hoffman et al, *The Alliance*

75 To see an example of Peer 1 Hosting's creatively designed office space that increased revenue, see Author unknown, 'Slide into Peer 1 Hosting's European headquarters', *Office Snapshots* (no date), https://officesnapshots.com/2013/05/15/peer-1-hosting-uk-office-design.

76 'Internet company opens "play" office', *BBC News* (10 April 2013), www.bbc.co.uk/news/av/uk-england-hampshire-22089159; Alexander, 'Yet another cool workplace', *The Chief Happiness Officer Blog* (20 January 2014), https://positivesharing.com/2014/01/yet-another-cool-workplace

77 For more information, see J Rossman, *Think Like Amazon: 50 1/2 ideas to become a digital leader* (McGraw Hill, 2019)

78 G Wickman, *Traction: Get a grip on your business* (BenBella Books, 2005); G Wickman, 'Effective meetings: Level 10 meeting for entrepreneurial leadership teams', EOS (no date), https://eosworldwide.com/blog/101916-thought-weekly-level-10-meeting-pure

79 Ray Dalio, *Principles: Life and Work* (Simon & Schuster, 2017)
80 J Collin, 'Vision framework: The Mars group' (2002), www. jimcollins.com/tools/vision-framework.pdf
81 N Karlinsky and J Stead, 'How a door became a desk, and a symbol of Amazon', *Amazon News* (17 April 2018), www. aboutamazon.eu/news/working-at-amazon/how-a-door-became-a-desk-and-a-symbol-of-amazon
82 For more on this, read James Kerr, *Legacy: What the All Blacks can teach us about the business of life* (Constable, 2013)
83 No author, 'Czech deer still avoid Iron Curtain', *BBC News* (23 April 2014), https://bbc.co.uk/news/world-europe-27129727
84 V Harnish, *Scaling Up: How a few companies make it… and why the rest don't* (Gazelles, 2014); V Harnish, *Mastering the Rockefeller Habits: What you must do to increase the value of your fast-growth firm* (Gazelles, 2002)
85 Shannon Byrne Susko, *3HAG Way: The strategic execution system that ensures your strategy is not a wild-ass-guess!* (Ceozen Consulting, 2018)
86 James L Heskett, *The Value Profit Chain: Treat employees like customers and customers like employees* (Free Press, 2014)
87 Henry Stewart, *The Happy Manifesto*

Acknowledgements

M any people have had a profound impact on my life.

Two people hired me when I had no discernible skills for the roles: Peter Birkett and Neil Jackson.

Thanks to Ken Austin at Glaxo. As part of his team 'Ken's Kamikazes' in the early days of my career, I learned so much about motivation and engagement. Thank you also to David Fish, whom I never worked for, but who shared with me his knowledge and time.

Morris Miller, Lanham Napier and Graham Weston were influential during my time at Rackspace, where I was also introduced to the work of Verne Harnish – specifically *Scaling Up* and *Mastering the Rockefeller*

Habits.[84] His methodology has been my guiding light ever since. It's no exaggeration to say that Verne has changed my life, so huge thanks to him!

It's also important to mention the work of Shannon Susko. Her book *3HAG Way* came at just the right time, giving me a great structure for coaching.[85]

Fabio Banducci and Gary Sherlock at Peer 1 Hosting were inspirational to work alongside. Our quarterly off-sites to work on our interpersonal relationships were so effective they inspired me to become a coach.

A huge thank you to every one of our *Melting Pot* podcast guests. Your insights continue to inspire me and enrich my coaching. Special mentions go to Fred Reichheld for inventing the brilliant NPS, Horst Schulze for inspiring us at Rackspace to follow in Ritz Carlton's footsteps and James Heskett for *Value Profit Chain*, which I still feel is the best business book I have ever read.[86] Also, Henry Stewart and his *Happy Manifesto* – he's been a fantastic mentor who helped me re-evaluate my beliefs and biases.[87]

This book wouldn't exist without the expert guidance of Lee Black from Speak It To Book. I'd also like to thank my brilliant team at Monkhouse & Company for their patience and support, especially Jo Coleman, who transforms my thoughts into words.

The Author

Dominic Monkhouse is the CEO and Founder of Monkhouse & Company, a no-bullsh*t coaching company that helps entrepreneurial CEOs and their leadership team reach their goals faster.

In the last two recessions (9/11 and GFC) Dominic has scaled two UK technology service firms to £30m annual run rate revenue within five years. He learned which execution systems worked, made plenty of mistakes, tried, tested and discarded other tools, and discovered innovative strategies that disrupted competitors. At Rackspace, they grew to 150 people on the team at £30m. At Peer 1 Hosting the team was 120 strong in the UK at £30m. The team went on to grow Peer 1 Hosting globally from $94m to $200m before exiting for $635m.

Since the early 2000s, Dominic has empowered many CEOs and their leadership teams. He has now created a purpose-built Management Lab on his farm in Wiltshire, where he shares the systems, tools and strategies that enabled him to scale. Billed as 'the happy entrepreneur', Dominic has been called 'Britain's Best Boss', has been cited in the Daily Telegraph as the creator of the 'best office in Britain', and has been welcomed on the BBC Breakfast show to talk about his work. He is also the author of *F**k Plan B*.

🌐 www.monkhouseandcompany.com

🔲 www.linkedin.com/in/dominicmonkhouse